Contemporary

Foundations

Science

Wright Group

www.WrightGroup.com

Copyright © 2009 by Wright Group/McGraw-Hill.

Send all inquiries to:
Wright Group/McGraw-Hill
P.O. Box 812960
Chicago IL 60681

ISBN: 978-1-4045-7636-0
MHID: 1-4045-7636-3

1 2 3 4 5 6 7 8 9 10 COU 12 11 10 09 08

CONTENTS

Contents

Introduction

Welcome to Contemporary's *Foundations: Science*. This book will help you understand science topics that affect your everyday life. You will practice reading science passages, trying your own experiments, and writing about what you have learned.

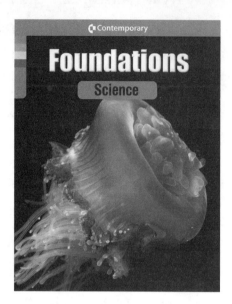

There are many branches of science. In this book, you will learn about five areas of science.

Human Biology—the study of how our bodies work

Plant Biology—the study of plants and how they grow

Physics—the study of topics such as energy, force, light, and sound

Chemistry—the study of what substances are made of and how substances can change

Earth Science—the study of Earth and how we can take care of it

These special features in *Foundations: Science* will help you learn the skills needed to understand science topics.

Try It Yourself!—simple experiments that will give you a better understanding of the topics you have been reading about

Writing Workshops—detailed instructions that will guide you through the four-step writing process: prewriting, drafting, revising, and editing

Language Tips—explanations, pronunciations, study hints, and background information that will help you understand what you are reading

Test Skills—a reminder that this skill is often tested on standardized tests

Posttest—a test, evaluation chart, and answer key so you will know how well you have mastered the skills

We hope you will enjoy *Foundations: Science*. We wish you the best of luck with your studies!

Foundations

Contemporary's *Foundations* is a series of books designed to help you improve your skills. Each book provides skill instruction, offers interesting passages to study, and gives opportunities to practice what you are learning.

In addition to *Foundations: Science*, we invite you to explore these books.

- In *Foundations: Math*, you will practice using **whole numbers, money, decimals, fractions, ratios,** and **percents**.
- Exercises will help you review the **addition, subtraction, multiplication,** and **division** facts; **round numbers; estimate** answers; and solve **word problems**.
- **Math Notes, On Your Calculator,** and **Language Tips** will help you improve your math skills.

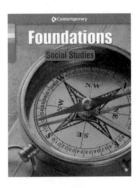

- In *Foundations: Social Studies*, you will learn about **world history, U.S. history, civics** and **government, geography,** and **economics**.
- You will **summarize,** make **predictions,** infer the main idea of **cartoons,** find information on **maps,** and read various kinds of **graphs**.
- **Background Information, Language Tips,** and **Writing Workshops** will let you use what you already know as you read and write about social studies topics.

- In *Foundations: Reading,* you will read **practical information, nonfiction, poetry,** and **short stories**.
- You will learn to find the **main point** and the **details;** identify **fact, opinion,** and **bias;** make **inferences;** read **photographs** and **cartoons;** and understand **rhythm, rhyme, plot,** and **theme**.
- **Writing Workshops, Language Tips,** and **prereading questions** will help you become a better reader, writer, and thinker.

- In *Foundations: Writing,* you will practice the four steps to writing an essay: **prewriting, drafting, revising,** and **editing**.
- You will read and write five kinds of essays—**descriptive essays, personal narratives, how-to essays, essays of example,** and **comparison-and-contrast essays**.
- A language-skills workbook gives you **grammar, punctuation,** and **sentence structure** practice.
- **In Your Journal, With a Partner,** and **Language Tips** will help you become a better writer—and a better reader and thinker.

UNIT 1
Human Biology

How is the human body put together? What does the body do to stay alive and healthy? Which illnesses can affect the body? These are some of the questions answered by a branch of science called **human biology**. Human biology helps us appreciate what our bodies do. It also helps us keep our bodies healthy.

Chapter	What You Will Learn About	What You Will Read
1	Finding Details	The Heart and Blood Pressure The S's of Physical Fitness Cholesterol: Too Much of a Good Thing How the Body Senses Pain
2	Finding the Main Idea	Parts of the Human Brain Give Your Hand a Hand Keeping Your Balance The Eyes Have It
3	Summarizing	Size *and* Bones Muscles, Taste, *and* Kidneys Height, Hair, Wrinkles, *and* Joints Shivering *and* Emotions
4	Putting Events in Sequence	In Your Dreams The Body's Air Conditioning *and* How to Mend a Broken Bone Follow the Food With Every Beat of Your Heart
5	Reading Diagrams	The Skull and the Spine The Respiratory System Skin Bone Fractures
Review	Human Biology	What Causes Tooth Decay?

After studying this unit, you should be able to

- find details and identify the main idea
- summarize important points
- put facts in sequence, or order
- read diagrams

Chapter 1

Finding Details

Finding details may not sound important, but we need to find details every day. For example, if a friend tells you about a job opening, you will ask for details: What kind of work is it? What are the hours? Where is the job? How much does it pay?

When you read about science, you will read facts that answer the questions *what? who? why? where? when?* or *how?* These facts are details. They explain the main subject of the reading so that you can understand what you are reading about.

As you read details, try to picture them in your mind. Picturing details will help you understand and remember them. If you have trouble picturing a detail, you may not have understood what you read. In that case, go back and read the information again.

Practice finding the details in the following passage. They are the facts that answer the questions *what? who? why? where? when?* or *how?* Try to form a mental picture of each detail.

The Heart and Blood Pressure

THE HEART AS A PUMP

Have you ever exercised hard and then suddenly stopped? If so, you may have heard a steady thumping in your ears. These thumps—which occur once or twice each second—are the sound of your blood flowing through your body. Your heart is the most powerful muscle in your body. Its job is to make your blood flow through your body.

Think about the action of the heart. Imagine what happens if you cup your hands together under water, leaving room between your hands for water. When you squeeze your hands together, you can squirt water into the air. The heart works in a similar way. It contracts (or squeezes) and relaxes, contracts and relaxes, never stopping. The heart keeps blood flowing through the tube-like blood vessels of the body.

As the blood flows through these vessels, it pushes against the vessel walls. This force is called blood pressure. When the heart contracts, it sends the blood rushing more quickly. Blood pressure increases. The pressure is strongest when the blood comes spurting out of the heart. Farther from the heart, the pressure is weaker. When the heart relaxes, the blood flows more slowly. Blood pressure then decreases.

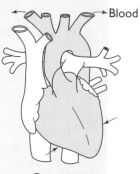

Contracting

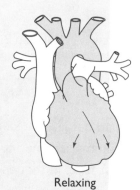

Relaxing

Answer these questions about the details in this passage.

1. How is the heart like a fist? (Hint: Read through paragraph 2.)

   _____

2. What is blood pressure? (Hint: Read paragraph 3.)

   _____

3. When the heart contracts, how does blood pressure change?

   _____

4. When the heart relaxes, how does blood pressure change?

   _____

You answers should have been similar to these:

1. The heart is like a fist because it can squeeze and relax.
2. Blood pressure is the force of blood pushing against the walls of blood vessels.
3. When the heart contracts, blood pressure increases. (This detail is found in paragraph 3.)
4. When the heart relaxes, blood pressure decreases. (This detail is found in paragraph 3.)

If your answers were correct, you probably did a good job of picturing the details.

Strategy: How to Find Details

- Ask the questions *what? who? why? where? when?* or *how?*
- Form a mental picture of the facts presented by the author.
- Think about how the facts help you understand the passage.

Exercise 1

When was the last time you had a sore back or a strained muscle? Are you physically fit? How can you tell?

Read the passage. Then circle the best answer for each question.

The S's of Physical Fitness

Physical fitness has three characteristics: suppleness, strength, and stamina.

Suppleness is the ability to bend and twist freely without great effort and without hurting yourself. In everyday life, you need suppleness to get out of bed, to sit, to stand, and to reach for things. If your body is supple, you are less likely to hurt yourself while exercising or doing everyday activities. You can also move more quickly if you are supple.

Strength is the power in one's muscles. Strength helps prevent strains or sprains when you lift, push, or pull things. Muscles support the backbone. Strong muscles are needed for good posture.

Stamina is the ability to work or exercise for a long period without getting tired. If you have stamina, you probably will not run out of breath quickly. You will not feel worn out while you work or exercise.

Healthy children who lead average, active lives generally have plenty of suppleness, strength, and stamina. Adults, however, must work harder to stay in good physical shape. Unless they exercise regularly, they will find that all three of these characteristics will decrease as they age.

1. *Suppleness* means
   (1) the power in one's muscles
   (2) the ability to work or exercise for a long time without getting tired
   (3) the ability to lead an active life
   (4) the ability to bend and twist freely

2. Suppleness helps you
   (1) lift heavy objects
   (2) move more quickly
   (3) have good posture
   (4) work longer without getting tired

3. Strength helps you to
   (1) move more quickly
   (2) sit, stand, or reach for things
   (3) exercise for a long period without getting tired
   (4) prevent strains or sprains

4. *Stamina* means
   (1) the power in one's muscles
   (2) the ability to work or exercise for a long time without getting tired
   (3) the ability to lead an active life
   (4) the ability to bend and twist freely

5. According to the passage, one difference between children and adults is that
   (1) children are stronger than adults
   (2) children are more supple than adults
   (3) adults have to work harder to stay physically fit
   (4) adults are stronger than children

Check your answers on page 192.

Exercise 2

LANGUAGE Tip

Some people remember the meaning of *LDL* and *HDL* by using these clues:

LDL is "lousy" cholesterol.

HDL is "happy" cholesterol.

Every organ in the body needs a constant supply of blood. If the blood flow is blocked, there is trouble. What stops the flow of blood? What can be done to prevent that from happening?

Read the passage and complete the exercise.

Cholesterol: Too Much of a Good Thing

Cholesterol is a waxy substance that floats in the blood. The liver produces cholesterol because the body needs cholesterol to keep its cells healthy. The liver usually makes the amount of cholesterol that the body needs. However, it may make more cholesterol than the body can use. In that case, cholesterol can be dangerous.

Cholesterol is carried in the bloodstream by **lipoproteins**. There are two major kinds of lipoproteins. They are called LDL and HDL.

LDL carries most of the cholesterol in the bloodstream. When the LDL has too much cholesterol to carry, cholesterol builds up inside the arteries. If it builds up enough, the flow of blood can be blocked. When blood to a person's heart is blocked, he or she may have a heart attack. When blood to the brain is blocked, the person may have a stroke.

Some doctors feel that HDL is useful. HDL seems to carry cholesterol to the liver. The liver then removes the cholesterol from the body. HDL may also help to break up blocks of cholesterol that have built up in the blood vessels. For these reasons, HDL cholesterol is sometimes called "good cholesterol."

It is important to control the amount of cholesterol in your blood. One way to control it is to watch what you eat. Avoid eating too many foods from animal sources. These foods contain cholesterol. They add cholesterol to the cholesterol that your body has already made. Instead, eat a diet low in animal fats and rich in vegetables and nuts. You can also control cholesterol by exercising regularly and by not smoking. Smoking lowers the amount of HDL, the "good cholesterol." Exercising raises HDL.

Circle the best answer for each question.

1. The human body makes cholesterol in the
   (1) stomach
   (2) brain
   (3) heart
   (4) liver

2. Too much cholesterol in the blood is a problem because cholesterol
   (1) keeps people from exercising properly
   (2) can build up in the arteries and block the flow of blood
   (3) takes away muscle strength
   (4) makes the blood move too fast through the arteries

3. LDL
   (1) carries most of the cholesterol in the bloodstream
   (2) carries less cholesterol than HDL
   (3) breaks up cholesterol blocks
   (4) is made by the liver

4. Many experts say that HDL cholesterol
   (1) should be at lower levels than LDL cholesterol levels
   (2) is more dangerous than LDL cholesterol
   (3) can be broken up by LDL cholesterol
   (4) is "good cholesterol"

5. Exercise is helpful in controlling cholesterol because it
   (1) raises the amount of LDL in the blood
   (2) lowers the desire to eat foods from animal sources
   (3) raises the amount of HDL in the blood
   (4) lowers the amount of LDL in the blood

Check your answers on page 192.

Exercise 3

What happens when your hand brushes against something hot and you suddenly jerk your hand away?

Read the passage. Then answer the questions.

LANGUAGE Tip

Suffixes

By adding endings to the word *sense*, you can form new words:
sensitive (able to feel)
sensation (a feeling)
sensor (a device that feels heat, light, etc.)

How the Body Senses Pain

When your skin touches something, what does it sense? Just below the surface of the skin are tiny organs that can sense touch, pressure, pain, and temperature. These organs are called receptors because they "receive" information. When the receptors sense something, they send a message to the brain. The brain registers a response such as "Ouch—that's hot!" or "Mmm—that's smooth and silky."

Some parts of the body are more sensitive than others. That is because different body parts have different numbers of pain receptors. For example, the eye has more pain receptors than most other parts of the body. The eye feels pain when it senses even a small amount of pressure. It would take 500 times as much pressure on the back of the hand to cause pain. It would take 1,500 times as much pressure on the fingertips to cause pain.

The eye's sensitivity to pain is useful. The eye is very delicate, and it can be easily injured. Pain receptors give us an early warning of dangers that may threaten our health or safety. They are the body's way of protecting itself from harm.

1. What are receptors? _____

2. What part of the body do receptors send messages to? _____

3. Why is the eye more sensitive than other parts of the body?

_____

4. How do pain receptors help us?

_____

Check your answers on page 192.

Try It Yourself!

In this chapter, you have learned about the tiny organs that sense temperature. Try this experiment to test how temperature affects the way your muscles move.

Hypothesis
(A hypothesis is a careful guess that helps explain facts.)
The ability of a muscle to work is affected by the temperature of the muscle.

Materials you will need
a small rubber ball
a bowl of ice water

Test it!
Count the number of times you can squeeze a rubber ball in 30 seconds. Do several trials, and record the results in a table like the one below.

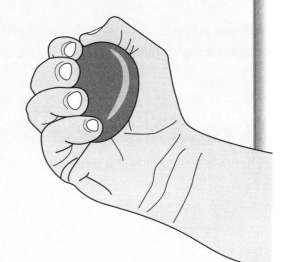

Trial	Number of Squeezes	
	Warm	**Cold**
1		
2		
3		
4		

Then place your hand in the ice water for 1 minute. (Do not leave your hand in the ice water so long that you feel uncomfortable.) Now repeat the trials.

Compare the results of warm-muscle trials with the results of cold-muscle trials. What do the results of this experiment tell you about working outside on cold days?

Check your results on page 192.

Chapter 2

Finding the Main Idea

Have you ever glanced at a newspaper and noticed the headline? Perhaps the headline was something like this:

Doctors Predict Flu Outbreak

Headlines give you a general idea about the **topic** of the article. The topic is the general subject of the article. Headlines are written to attract your attention so you will want to read the whole article.

The first sentence in a newspaper article usually states the **main idea**. The main idea is the most important point of the story. It sums up all of the details.

In a well-written article, each paragraph has a main idea. Sometimes the main idea is clearly stated, often in the first sentence of the paragraph. However, sometimes the writer does not clearly state the main idea of a paragraph. Then you have to figure out the main idea.

Below is a passage about the brain. Read the passage. Then read on to learn more about the main idea and the details.

Parts of the Human Brain

(1) We often think of the brain as a single organ. (2) However, your brain has three main parts. (3) The largest part is the **cerebral cortex**. (4) Its job is to learn, reason, and remember. (5) It also helps you understand and use the messages that your senses send to your brain. (6) <u>Whenever you need to think and react, your cerebral cortex goes into action.</u>

(7) The two other parts of the brain quietly keep your body systems going. (8) The **cerebellum** controls balance and movements such as walking. (9) The **brain stem** is in charge of basic needs such as breathing, digesting, and sleeping.

Look at the first paragraph of the passage. Do you see that the last sentence states the main idea of the paragraph? The other sentences provide details about what the cerebral cortex is and how it helps you think and react.

Now look at the second paragraph of the passage. Which sentence expresses the main idea of this paragraph?

If you said **sentence 7**, you are correct.

Now think about the whole passage. Read the main-idea sentence of each paragraph. Then write a sentence that states the main idea of the whole passage.

Main idea of the passage: _____

_____

Your sentence should say something like this: *The cerebral cortex helps you think and react, while the cerebellum and the brain stem control basic body systems.* This sentence ties together all the details of the passage.

Strategy: How to Find the Main Idea

- Read the passage.
- Identify the topic. The topic tells *who* or *what* the passage is about.
- To find the main idea of the passage, ask yourself, "What main point does the author make about the topic?"
- If a passage has more than one paragraph, look for the main idea of each paragraph. Then find the main point of the whole passage.
- To check that you have found the main idea, ask yourself these questions:
    - "Is this the author's most important idea?"
    - "Do all the details in the passage explain or describe the main idea?"

Exercise 1

What are three things you can do with your hands that other animals cannot do with their paws? Why do you suppose hands can do so much more than paws can?

Read the passage and then complete the exercise.

LANGUAGE Tip

Prefix

The prefix *fore-* means "before." Your **forearm** comes before your upper arm. Your **forehead** is the part of your face that is above your eyes.

Give Your Hand a Hand

Most of us take our hands for granted. We are not surprised when they do the tasks we expect them to do. In reality, the human hand is a truly amazing tool.

The human hand has 27 bones. It has 34 muscles that move the fingers and thumb. These muscles are not in the fingers and thumbs. They are in the palm of the hand and in the forearm. The muscles pull **tendons** in the hand. The tendons, in turn, pull the fingers. In a way, the fingers move by remote control. (Look at the back of your hand as you wiggle your fingers. You will see your tendons pulling at the fingers.)

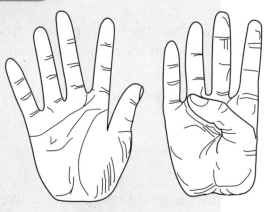

Opposable Thumb

With its strong bones and muscles, the human hand can do jobs that demand strength. For example, mountain climbers use their hands to grip rocks as they pull themselves up the side of a mountain. Carpenters squeeze nail guns to nail boards together.

The human hand is different from the paws or hands of most other animals. Only apes and monkeys have hands that are similar to ours. That is because they, like humans, have opposable thumbs. An **opposable** thumb can move across the palm to meet the other four fingers on the hand. This ability gives the human hand a grip that is able to move, turn, and twist as needed. Because of its special opposable thumb, the human hand can do a variety of tasks. The hand has the strength to grip and squeeze. It also has enough control to do fine or delicate work. For example, the human hand can pick up a dime or sew tiny stitches.

Today is a good day to be grateful for the wonderful tool we depend on every day—the hand.

1. What is the topic of the whole passage?
   (1) bones and muscles
   (2) human beings and other animals
   (3) the human hand
   (4) mountain climbing

2. Which sentence best states the main idea of paragraph 2?
   (1) The human hand has 27 bones.
   (2) There are 34 muscles that move the fingers and thumb.
   (3) Muscles in the palm and forearm control the fingers and thumb.
   (4) Tendons move muscles in your hand.

3. According to the passage, what makes the human hand different from the hands or paws of most other animals?
   (1) The human hand has more bones.
   (2) The human hand needs more muscles to move.
   (3) The human hand is larger than the hand or paw of any other animal.
   (4) The human hand has an opposable thumb.

4. What makes the opposable thumb especially useful?
   (1) It allows humans to do fine work.
   (2) It is just like the hands of apes and monkeys.
   (3) About 34 muscles are needed to make it move.
   (4) It makes the human hand stronger than apes' hands.

5. Which sentence best states the main idea of the whole passage?
   (1) Opposable thumbs set humans apart from all other animals.
   (2) The human hand is an amazing tool that can do many things.
   (3) The human hand has 27 bones and 34 muscles.
   (4) There are no muscles in the fingers and thumbs of a human hand.

Check your answers on page 192.

Exercise 2

If you go on a ride that spins you around, why do you lose your balance? What keeps you standing even though you feel unsteady? How does your body stand up against forces that are working on it?

Read the passage and then complete the exercise.

Keeping Your Balance

Keeping your balance is harder than think. Your brain needs information from three sources to keep your body upright.

Your eyes give the brain one kind of information. The brain wants to know answers to questions such as these: Am I right-side up or upside down? Am I leaning to the left or to the right? What forces are pushing against me? The eyes send messages to the brain about what they see. With this information, the brain can help you move your body so you do not fall.

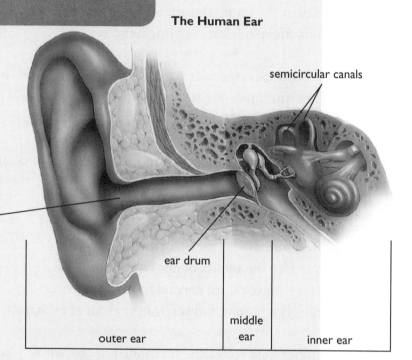

The Human Ear

semicircular canals

ear canal

ear drum

outer ear

middle ear

inner ear

The ear also sends balance information to the brain. The **semicircular canals** in the inner ear contain fluid. If you begin to fall, this fluid moves. A message then goes to the brain, and the brain sends urgent orders to the muscles to stop the fall. You may have noticed that you have trouble keeping your balance when you first get out of bed. That is because the fluid in your inner ear is moving around. It is sending messages to your brain. To keep you from falling, the brain must work quickly.

The third source of information is your muscles, joints, and skin. These body parts sense where you are. They sense the kind of surface your feet are touching. They sense how far your body is from objects such as furniture. Then, like your eyes and ears, they send messages to the brain so you will stay upright.

If any one of these sources of information fails, you may find you are no longer on your feet.

1. According to the passage, which body part has a fluid that senses when you are falling and then sends a message to your brain?
   (1) the eye
   (2) the muscles
   (3) the ear
   (4) the joints

2. Which sentence best expresses the main idea of paragraph 3?
   (1) The semicircular canals in the inner ear contain fluid.
   (2) The semicircular canals in your ear help you maintain balance.
   (3) Fluid in the ear sloshes around when you move quickly.
   (4) Your semicircular canals control your muscles.

3. Which sentence best expresses the main idea of paragraph 4?
   (1) Muscles, joints, and skin send information to the brain about where your body is.
   (2) Muscles, joints, and skin can tell what kind of surface your feet are on.
   (3) Muscles, joints, and skin sense where your body is.
   (4) Muscles, joints, and skin are not as important as the eyes and ears in helping you keep your balance.

4. Which sentence best expresses the main idea of the whole passage?
   (1) It is difficult to keep your balance, especially when you first get out of bed.
   (2) The ear is the most important organ for keeping your balance.
   (3) If you can see where you are going, you are more likely to keep your balance.
   (4) Information from your eyes, ears, muscles, joints, and skin helps your brain keep you balanced.

Check your answers on page 192.

Exercise 3

If you stare at something for a long time without blinking, your eyes will gradually become moist. Eventually the moisture will spill over and drip down your cheeks as tears. But if you blink, the moisture will probably disappear before it spills over as tears. Why is this?

Read the passage. Then circle the best answer for each question.

The Eyes Have It

Our eyes are constantly bathed by a salty liquid called tear fluid. This fluid is essential for keeping our eyes healthy. It sweeps away the dust or dirt that can damage our delicate eyes. Tear fluid also contains a chemical that helps kill germs and prevent infection.

Tear fluid is produced by almond-shaped organs called tear glands. These glands are found behind the upper eyelid. They pour fluid down onto the eye. This fluid eventually collects in the inner corner of the eye.

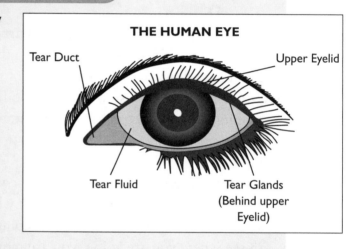

THE HUMAN EYE

Tear Duct

Upper Eyelid

Tear Fluid

Tear Glands
(Behind upper
Eyelid)

On the inside of the upper eyelid, near the inner corner of the eye, are two tiny holes. These holes are the entrances to the tear ducts. Tear fluid passes through the tear ducts and moves out of the eye. Each time the eyelid blinks, tear fluid is cleaned off the surface of the eye and swept into the tear duct. Eyelids are actually "windshield wipers." They endlessly clean tear fluid, dust, and dirt off the eye.

1. Which sentence best expresses the main idea of the first paragraph?
    (1) Eyes are always producing tear fluid.
    (2) Tear fluid contains a chemical.
    (3) Tear fluid helps protect the eyes.
    (4) Eyes are easily hurt by dust or dirt.

2. Which sentence best expresses the main idea of paragraph 3?
   (1) Tear fluid drains off the eye through the tear ducts.
   (2) Blinking sweeps tear fluid off the eye and into the tear ducts.
   (3) Blinking keeps dust and dirt out of the eyes.
   (4) Blinking closes the tear ducts and keeps tears from spilling over.

3. Which sentence best expresses the main idea of the passage?
   (1) Tear fluid helps prevent infection in our eyes.
   (2) Tear fluid is produced by tear glands.
   (3) The eyelids act as windshield wipers for our eyes.
   (4) Tear fluid cleans dirt from our eyes and is swept away by our eyelids.

Check your answers on page 192.

Try It Yourself!

In this chapter, you have learned how the eyelids act as windshield wipers to protect the eyes. Try this experiment to learn more about your eyes.

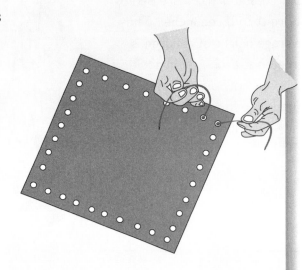

Hypothesis
Two eyes give better vision than one eye.

Materials you will need
a piece of cardboard with holes around its edge
a string
an eye patch

Test it!
Cover your left eye. Thread the string from one hole to another, going completely around the cardboard. Keep a record of how long it takes you.

Now uncover your eye and repeat the experiment.

You can continue this experiment by trying it again, this time with your right eye covered.

Was it quicker to work with one eye or two? Which way was easier? Write down what you found out.

Check your results on page 192.

Chapter 3

Summarizing

After reading a passage, you may want to summarize it. **Summarizing** is briefly retelling the important points of a passage in your own words. You summarize when you tell someone what happened in a story or a movie.

Summarizing can help you when you are reading science passages. Briefly retelling the important facts will help you remember what you read.

Read the following paragraph. Think about how you would summarize it.

Size

Over the past 100 years, the average height of adults in the United States has increased by more than three inches. The average height of children is greater at each age. In addition, children now become more mature at younger ages than they did 100 years ago.

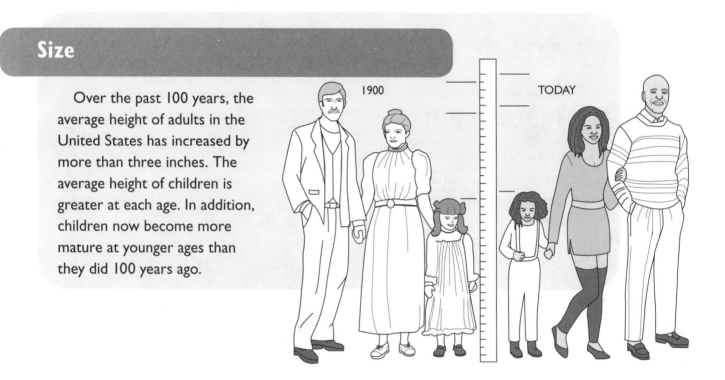

Read the following statements. Which is the best summary of the paragraph?

(1) Today Americans tend to be taller than they were 100 years ago.
(2) American children grow up faster than they did 100 years ago.
(3) Over the past 100 years, Americans have grown taller and have begun maturing at an earlier age.

Sentences (1) and (2) are true. However, each sentence summarizes only one fact presented in the paragraph. Sentence (3) is a good summary. It briefly retells all the important points of the paragraph.

Now read this paragraph.

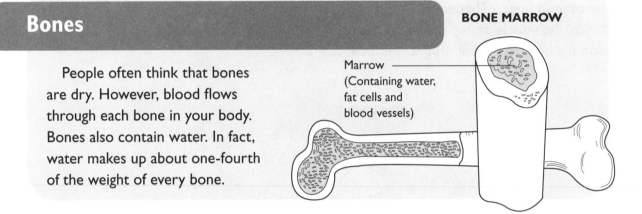

Bones

People often think that bones are dry. However, blood flows through each bone in your body. Bones also contain water. In fact, water makes up about one-fourth of the weight of every bone.

BONE MARROW

Marrow (Containing water, fat cells and blood vessels)

Write a sentence that summarizes this paragraph.

_____

_____

To retell the most important points in the paragraph, your summary should say something like this: *Bones are not dry, for they contain blood and water.* This sentence sums up all the important points in the paragraph about bones.

Strategy: How to Summarize

- Note the key ideas or details.
- Ask, "What is the main point? Which details are most important?"
- To check that you have written a good summary, ask yourself, "Does this statement retell all the important points?"

Exercise 1

Read each paragraph. Then circle the best answer for each question.

LANGUAGE Tip

muscle   MUH sil
Notice that the *c* in this word is not pronounced.

Muscles

The muscles that help us move are attached to bones. Muscles can only pull bones; they cannot push bones. Therefore, most muscles work in pairs. To bend your arm, for instance, the muscle on top of your arm pulls it up. To straighten your arm, the muscle on the bottom of your arm pulls it back down.

ARM MUSCLES

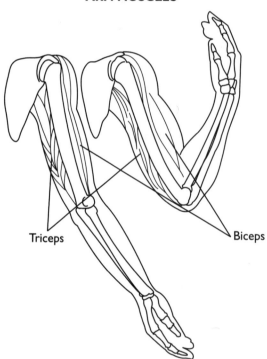

Triceps   Biceps

1. Which is the best summary of these facts?
    (1) The arm has one muscle on the top and another muscle on the bottom.
    (2) Most muscles are attached to bones, such as the arm bones.
    (3) Because muscles can only pull, they work in pairs to move bones.
    (4) The muscles of the arm can move the arm either up or down.

Taste

The tiny bumps on your tongue, called taste buds, pick up signals from the food you eat. There are only four different taste signals—sweet, sour, salty, and bitter. The taste buds on the outer edges of the tongue sense sour tastes. The taste buds on the back of the tongue sense bitterness. Taste buds on the tip of the tongue sense both sweetness and saltiness.

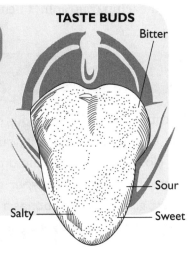

TASTE BUDS
Bitter
Sour
Salty
Sweet

2. Which is the best summary of these facts?
   (1) Sweet, sour, salty, and bitter tastes are sensed by taste buds on different parts of your tongue.
   (2) The tiny bumps on the tongue are taste buds that can sense four different taste signals.
   (3) Taste buds are located on four different parts of the tongue.
   (4) All tastes are actually made up of only four different signals—sweet, sour, salty, and bitter.

Kidneys

The kidneys are bean-shaped organs located near the lower back. They clean waste materials from the blood. These wastes, together with extra water, then leave the body in the form of urine. In this way, the kidneys help keep conditions stable inside the body.

3. Which is the best summary of these facts?
   (1) Water and waste products leave the body.
   (2) The kidneys clean waste materials from the blood.
   (3) The kidneys are organs that help keep the body stable by cleaning waste products from the blood.
   (4) The kidneys help keep the body stable.

Check your answers on page 192.

Exercise 2

Read each paragraph. Then circle the best answer for each question.

Height

Gravity has an effect on your height each day. In the morning, you are your full height. During the day, gravity pulls the bones of your spine down and moves the bones closer together. By the time you go to bed at night, you are about one inch shorter. Then as you lie in your bed at night, gravity stops pulling down on your spine. This rest gives the spine bones a chance to move farther apart again. You start the next day at your full height again.

1. Which sentence is the best summary of these facts?
   (1) Gravity pulls your spine bones closer during the day, but you regain your height when the bones move farther apart.
   (2) Because of gravity, you lose one inch of height each day.
   (3) The bones of your spine move so your height changes during the day.
   (4) Each morning you are about one inch taller than you were when you went to bed the night before.

Hair

You can tell whether a hair is straight or curly even if you have only a small piece of the hair. Look at the end of the strand under a microscope. If the end is round, your hair is straight. If the strand has an oval shape, your hair is wavy. If it is shaped like a flattened oval, your hair is curly.

2. Which sentence is the best summary of these facts?
   (1) If you look at a strand of hair under a microscope, you can tell how curly the hair is.
   (2) Under a microscope, a straight hair looks round, a wavy hair looks oval, and a curly hair looks like a flattened oval.
   (3) If you change the shape of each hair, you can make your hair curlier.
   (4) If people have straight hair, their hairs are round.

Wrinkles

Your skin has oils that make it waterproof. However, when you soak in a warm bath for a long time, these oils wash away. Then water can seep through the skin. Some of the skin absorbs the water and puffs up. Skin that is firmly connected to what is below it does not absorb water. This skin does not puff up. Because some of your skin is puffed up and some is not, your skin looks wrinkled.

3. Which sentence is the best summary of these facts?
   (1) Some skin is firmly attached to what is below it.
   (2) Staying in bath water too long causes skin to wrinkle.
   (3) Oils protect the skin from drying out most of the time, but staying in the bath too long washes the oils away.
   (4) Your skin appears wrinkled when some skin absorbs water and some skin does not.

Joints

Your body is designed to move. Joints connect your bones in a variety of ways so you can do various kinds of movements. The bones in your knees, elbows, and fingers are connected with hinge joints. These joints move back and forth, much like the hinges on a door. The bones in your shoulders and hips are connected with ball-and-socket joints. One bone has a ball on the end of it. The other bone has a cup-like hole that the ball fits into. These joints let you move your shoulders and hips in almost any direction. The bones in your neck are connected by pivot joints. They let you turn your head.

4. Which sentence is the best summary of these facts?
   (1) In order for the body to move, the bones must be movable.
   (2) Ball-and-socket joints give you the greatest movement.
   (3) Hinge joints, ball-and-socket joints, and pivot joints let the body move in different ways.
   (4) The body is designed in a remarkable way.

Check your answers on page 192.

In most science writing, facts are presented in paragraphs, not in lists. Sometimes each sentence states a new fact.

Read each paragraph. Then circle the best answer for each question.

Shivering

When your body gets cold, your muscles squeeze together. Then your muscles quickly relax. This is what we call shivering. When muscles squeeze and relax over and over, they produce heat. The heat helps warm up your body.

1. Which is the best summary of the facts in this paragraph?
   (1) Shivering is an activity of the muscles.
   (2) The human body can adjust to cold temperatures.
   (3) When muscles move, they produce heat.
   (4) Shivering, the rapid squeezing and relaxing of muscles, helps keep the body warm.

Emotions

When you feel a strong emotion such as anger or embarrassment, your heart may start beating faster. This sends more blood rushing through your body. As a result, the skin on your face may suddenly look darker. That is what we call blushing.

2. Which is the best summary of the facts in this paragraph?
   (1) Blushing is what people notice when there is more blood in the face.
   (2) Blushing occurs when strong emotion makes the heart beat faster and pump more blood.
   (3) Blushing can happen when you feel a strong emotion.
   (4) When the heart pumps faster, it sends more blood through the body.

Check your answers on page 192.

Try It Yourself!

In this chapter, you have learned how your taste buds sense different tastes. Try this experiment to learn more about how your other senses help you identify foods.

Hypothesis
The senses of taste, smell, and sight work together to help you identify food.

Materials you will need
an apple, a pear, a potato, a sweet potato, and a carrot
toothpicks
blindfold

Test it!
Wash your hands thoroughly, and then peel several fruits and vegetables such as an apple, a pear, a potato, a sweet potato, and a carrot. Cut samples of each food into ½-inch cubes. Put a toothpick in each cube.

Blindfold someone. Put cubes of food near the person's nose and ask the person to try to identify each food by its smell. Then have the person taste the samples and try to identify the foods. Finally, remove the blindfold and ask the person to look at the samples and identify them.

You can continue this experiment by testing several people. You can change the experiment by using flavored jelly beans or other foods.

Make a chart to summarize your findings. Tell how the person correctly identified foods. Use the chart below as an example.

	Apple	**Pear**	**Potato**	**Sweet Potato**	**Carrot**
Person 1	taste, sight	smell, taste, sight	taste, sight	sight	taste, sight
Person 2					

Check your results on page 192.

Chapter 4

Putting Events in Sequence

When you study science, you often read descriptions of how things happen. Here are a few of the many processes that are taking place every moment inside your body.

The lungs expand to take in air.
The heart pumps blood through the body.
The blood picks up oxygen from the lungs.

During each of these processes, one thing happens and then another and then another. When you read a description of a process, you need to understand the **sequence** in which things happen. The sequence is the time order in which events occur.

Read the following paragraph. It describes the common process of dreaming.

In Your Dreams

What happens when you go to sleep? Usually you first fall into a light sleep. During this stage, it would be easy for someone to wake you. Within a few minutes, you begin to dream. A dream lasts for a few minutes and then it ends.

Did you notice words in the passage that signaled the time when things happened? The words *first, within a few minutes, for a few minutes,* and *then* help you figure out the order of events. If you listed all the events in this paragraph in the order in which they happen, your list would look like this:

1. You fall into a light sleep.
2. You begin to dream.
3. The dream lasts a few minutes.
4. The dream ends.

Now read this paragraph. It describes what happens after the first dream ends.

When the first dream is over, you fall into a deep sleep. About an hour and a half later, you have another dream. It is longer than the first dream. As long as you stay asleep, you will have a dream about every hour and a half.

Can you figure out the sequence of events in the paragraph? Underline all the words that signal sequence, or time order, in the paragraph.

Write down what happens right after the first dream ends.

_____

If you wrote *You fall into a deep sleep,* you were right.

Now write down when the next event happens and what that event is.

_____

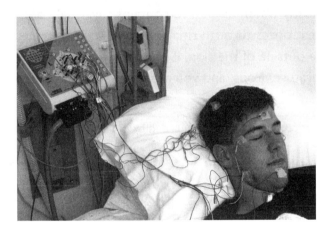

You should have written *An hour and a half later, you have another dream.*

As you read, watch for words like these. They signal the order of events.

first, second, third	then	afterward
next	later	in the meantime
before	last	today
after	finally	now

Strategy: How to Put Events in Sequence

- Look for words that signal time order, or sequence.
- Underline each event.
- Number the events in the order in which they happened.

Exercise 1

Read the passages and complete the exercise.

LANGUAGE Tip

Vowel Sounds

The vowel pair *ea* can be pronounced in several ways.

sw**ea**t	SWET
b**ea**t	BEET
gr**ea**t	GRAYT
d**ea**r	DIR

The Body's Air Conditioning

The body has an efficient way to cool itself down. We call this process sweating. When you exercise, you may get hot. Nerves in your skin sense the increased heat. They send messages to your brain saying that your skin temperature has increased. After the brain receives these messages, it sends messages to the sweat **glands**. The job of the millions of sweat glands in your skin is to produce sweat.

The sweat glands immediately begin to make sweat so you will cool you down. What we call sweat is mostly water, but it also contains sugar, salt, and some other chemicals. Next, the sweat oozes through small openings in your skin called pores. When sweat reaches the outside of the skin, it dries up. As it dries, it cools the skin. Finally, your body temperature drops, and you are much more comfortable.

glands: a part of the body that produces substances needed by other parts of the body

1. Number the events in order, from 1 to 5.
   _____ Nerves in your skin send warning messages to the brain.
   _____ The sweat glands produce sweat.
   _____ You exercise enough to get hot.
   _____ The brain sends messages telling the sweat glands to produce sweat.
   _____ The sweat oozes through pores and dries on your skin to cool it.

2. Complete the sentences below to describe what each body part does to keep you cool.
   (a) Nerves in the skin tell the brain that _____.
   (b) The brain reacts by _____.
   (c) When the sweat _____, it cools the body down.

How to Mend a Broken Bone

When you break a bone, your body springs into action. First, it sends blood to the site of the break. Soon a blood **clot**, a jellylike collection of blood cells, forms a bridge between the broken ends of the bone. Next, bone cells begin the task of removing dead bone material. Other bone cells start to make new bone material. In time, these new cells replace the clot with a temporary connector called a **callus**. The callus completely surrounds the break, acting like a collar. This collar makes the bone a little thicker than normal at site of the break.

Once the callus is complete, bone cells begin the process of turning the callus into hard bone. Slowly the callus disappears, and new bone material takes its place. Finally the new material reshapes itself until it is the same thickness as the bone was before the break. The newly made bone blends with the old bone parts to make a strong new bone.

The entire mending process usually takes four to six weeks. The exact time varies, depending on the type of break and the type of bone.

3. Number the events in order, from 1 to 5.
   _____ The new bone material reshapes itself so that it is the same thickness as the original bone parts.
   _____ A blood clot forms between the two bone parts.
   _____ Bone cells turn the callus into hard bone.
   _____ The bone breaks.
   _____ A callus replaces the blood clot.

4. List six words or phrases in the passage that signal sequence.

   _____   _____

   _____   _____

   _____   _____

Check your answers on page 193.

Exercise 2

Read the passage and complete the exercise.

LANGUAGE Tip

Use this pronunciation guide as you read this passage.

saliva	suh LI vuh
enzymes	EN zlmz
esophagus	i SAH fuh guhs

Follow the Food

How long does it take you to move three feet? You can probably cover that distance in one large step. But it takes the food you eat about two days to move that same distance. During that time, the food is battered, pushed, and churned. Finally it is digested or discarded. Follow along on the trip the food takes through your body.

First, you put the food into your mouth. There it is chewed and ground into small pieces. Saliva, which contains **enzymes**, begins the task of breaking the food into substances that your body can use.

The wet food then enters the esophagus. The esophagus is a tube made of strong muscles. It pushes the food down to the next stop on the journey, the stomach.

Your stomach is much like a cave. There the food is churned and mixed with acids and enzymes. It is the job of the acids to kill germs in the food. The enzymes continue to break down the food into useful chemicals. After the stomach does its work, the food is a liquid. It looks somewhat like lumpy soup.

This lumpy soup passes on to another tube, the small intestine. This tube, however, is not like the short, straight esophagus. The small intestine is about twenty feet long. It looks like a coil. This is the last place where enzymes work on digesting the food. The parts of the food that the body can use seep into your blood through the walls of the small intestine. The leftovers that your body does not need are sent to the large intestine.

Now the journey is complete. In the muscular tube called the large intestine, unneeded waste from the food you ate is stored until it is eliminated it from your body.

THE DIGESTIVE SYSTEM

Teeth
Mouth
Tongue
Salivary Glands
Esophagus
Stomach
Large Intestine
Small Intestine

---

enzymes: chemicals that speed up digestion

1. Number the events in order, from 1 to 5.

   _____ Food is pushed down the esophagus.

   _____ Substances needed from the food seep through the walls of the small intestine.

   _____ Waste from the food is stored in the large intestine.

   _____ Saliva begins to break the food down into substances the body can use.

   _____ The stomach churns the food and continues the process of breaking it down.

2. The first place where enzymes work with food is the
   (1) mouth
   (2) esophagus
   (3) stomach
   (4) large intestine

3. Partly digested food travels to the stomach through the
   (1) mouth
   (2) esophagus
   (3) small intestine
   (4) large intestine

4. The stomach's most important job is to
   (1) carry the food from the small intestine to the large intestine
   (2) combine food with acids and enzymes and mix it all up
   (3) store the unneeded waste until it is eliminated from the body
   (4) grind food into small pieces and combine it with saliva

5. Food goes into the small intestine just after
   (1) the esophagus pushes it down
   (2) unneeded waste is stored, ready to be eliminated
   (3) saliva begins to work on the food
   (4) the stomach turns the food into a soupy liquid

6. The last stop of the unneeded food on its journey through the body is the
   (1) stomach
   (2) mouth
   (3) large intestine
   (4) small intestine

Check your answers on page 193.

Exercise 3

In Chapter 1, you read about the heart as a pump. Where does the blood go after the heart pumps it?

Read the passage. Then complete the chart showing the course of the blood through the body.

With Every Beat of Your Heart

Place your hand on your chest. You should feel the steady thump-thump of your heart at work. The heart's job is to pump blood to every part of your body. Through each hour of life, this flow of blood never stops. That is because blood brings to each cell the oxygen and other substances that cells must have to stay alive.

Like a stock car on a race track, the blood follows one and only one route. It never strikes off on a new path, and it never makes a U-turn.

To trace the path of the blood, imagine starting inside the heart. The heart contracts (squeezes), forcing the blood into the lungs. Inside the lungs, the blood picks up oxygen. Oxygen turns the blood bright red.

The blood now circles back to the heart. The heart pumps the blood out again. This time, the blood goes to all other parts of the body. It delivers oxygen and other "food" that the cells must have. As the blood gives out all its oxygen, it turns dark reddish blue.

Now the blood has finished its delivery. It returns to the heart. There it begins the cycle once again. The blood is pumped to the lungs to pick up a new supply of oxygen.

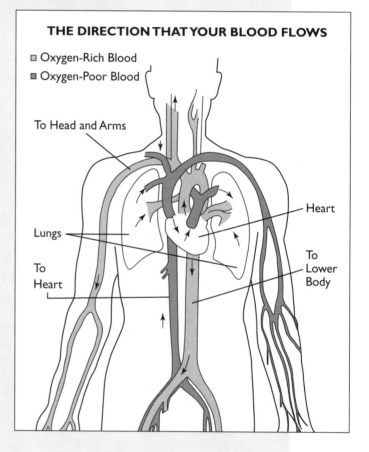

THE DIRECTION THAT YOUR BLOOD FLOWS

□ Oxygen-Rich Blood
■ Oxygen-Poor Blood

To Head and Arms
Lungs
To Head
Heart
To Lower Body

The Path of the Blood

Blood travels from the heart to

_____ *the lungs* _____, where the blood does these two things:

(1) _____

(2) _____ .

Then, it travels to

(3) _____ and to (4) _____,

where the blood does these two things: (5) _____

(6) _____ .

Finally, it travels to

(7) _____, where the blood (8) _____ .

Check your answers on page 193.

Writing Workshop

Prewriting
Think about a time when you had a medical problem. What did you do about it? Then what happened? Jot down answers to these questions. Choose the ideas you want to include in an essay. Finally, number the ideas to show the correct sequence of events.

Drafting
Write a few paragraphs, using your notes. Add time-order words between the events.

Revising
Read your essay to a partner. Ask your partner to write down the events in order. If your partner misses any of the events, revise to make the sequence clearer.

Editing
Capitalize all the words that name of a specific place, such as *Walker Sleep Laboratory*.

Chapter 5

Reading Diagrams

If you are driving to a new place, you might study a map to find out how to get there. A map is a type of **diagram**. It is a drawing of roads, highways, and other landmarks.

When you study science, you see many diagrams. Some diagrams show how the parts of something fit together. Other diagrams show how a process takes place.

You have probably heard the saying "a picture is worth a thousand words." This is certainly true in science. It is often easier to understand something by studying a diagram than by reading about it. Of course, this is true only if you know how to "read" diagrams. To read a map, you use the key to understand symbols, colors, and distances. In the same way, you need to use clues to read a scientific diagram.

The Skull and the Spine

THE BONES OF THE HEAD

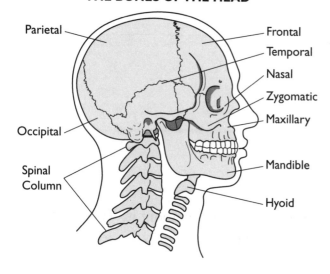

Look at the diagram. The first clue you should notice is the title. The title tells you the topic of the diagram: the bones of the head.

Now study the diagram closely. Notice the outline of a face as it is seen from one side. The nose is to the right, and the back of the head is to the left. You can identify the teeth, the eyes, and the backbone. You need to notice these details to understand where all the bones are in the head.

By studying the diagram closely, you can also learn some important facts. Do you see the jagged lines between many of the bones? These lines show how the bones of the head fit together. There is almost no space between these bones.

Finally, look at the **labels**. In this diagram, the labels are the names of the bones. Lines point from the labels to the various bones that they name.

◆ **Practice reading the diagram. Which bone is in the front of your throat?**

The label in front of the neck shows the answer: the *hyoid* bone.

What is the name of the two bones that the teeth grow in?

_____

If you wrote *maxillary and mandible*, you are right.

Study the diagram below. Which bones connect the head bones to the rest of the body? The answer is the *spinal column*. Notice that the spinal column is labeled differently from the bones in the last diagram. Instead of one straight line, the spinal column is marked with a bracket.

THE SPINAL COLUMN

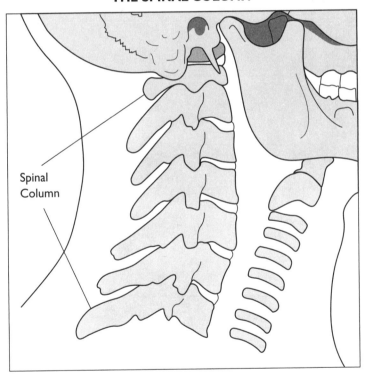

Spinal Column

The bracket points out several bones that are part of the spinal column. The name "spinal column" refers to all of those bones, not just one of them.

In fact, this diagram shows only part of the spinal column. If you looked at a diagram of the whole spinal column, you would see that it is made up of many more bones. The spinal column stretches all the way down your back.

Strategy: **How to Read Diagrams**

- Read the title. It tells what the diagram is about.
- Study the drawing. Look closely at the details.
- Read all the labels. They tell you what the pictures show.

Exercise 1

How does your body get the oxygen it needs?

Study the diagram and read the passage. Then answer the questions.

LANGUAGE Tip

Homophones

What is the difference between a **sac** and a **sack**?

A sac is part of a plant or an animal. It looks like a pocket.

A sack is a bag made of paper, plastic, or cloth.

The Respiratory System

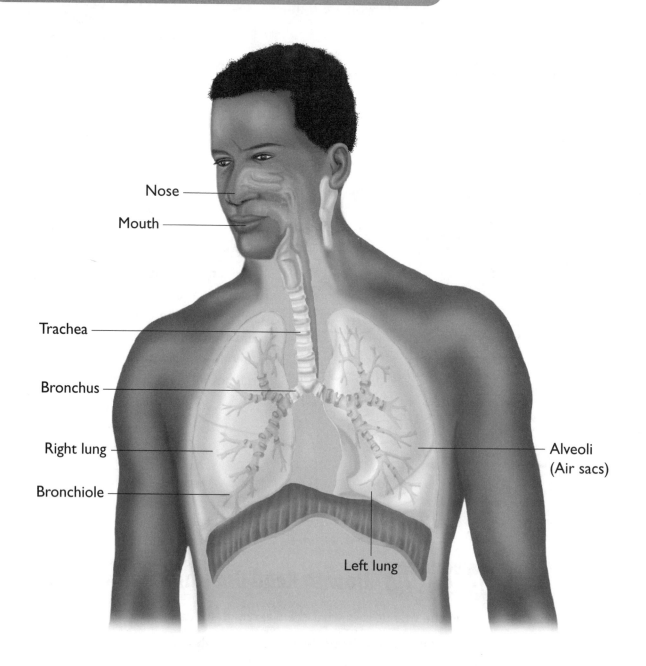

Nose

Mouth

Trachea

Bronchus

Right lung

Bronchiole

Alveoli (Air sacs)

Left lung

When **organs**[1] of the body work together, they form a **system**.[2] These systems perform the tasks that are needed to keep us alive.

For instance, humans need oxygen to survive. The respiratory system works to get oxygen to the blood. We breathe in air. Air travels to the lungs, where it ends up in tiny air sacs. Oxygen then moves from these air sacs into the blood.

The diagram shows the parts of the respiratory system.

---

[1]**organs:** cells and tissues that perform a certain task in the body; examples of organs are the heart, the lungs, and the brain

[2]**system:** a group of organs that work together to perform a major job such as breathing

1. From which *two* places can fresh air enter the trachea?

   _____

2. When the trachea divides into two branches, what is each branch called?

   _____

3. When the bronchus divides into smaller branches, what is each of the smaller branches called?

   _____

4. What is another name for *air sacs*?

   _____

5. According to the drawing, is there any major difference between the two lungs?

   _____

Check your answers on page 193.

Exercise 2

Skin, the body's largest organ, protects our bodies. Its structure also helps keep the temperature of the body stable. Can you guess how?

Study the diagram and read the passage. Then answer the questions.

Skin

THE STRUCTURE OF HUMAN SKIN

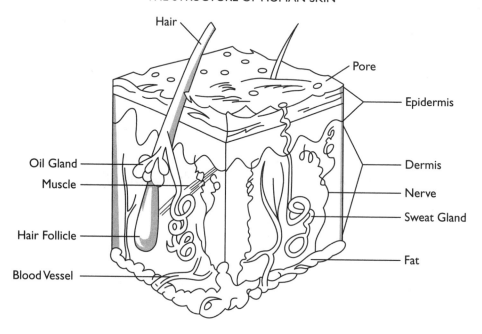

When our bodies get too hot, extra blood flows to the skin. The sweat glands work to take saltwater and other wastes from the blood. This mixture is called **perspiration**. When perspiration flows out of the skin, the body cools.

When our bodies are cold, less blood flows to the skin. This prevents the blood from losing too much heat. The body keeps its heat inside.

The diagram shows the structure of skin.

1. The two layers of the skin are the epidermis and the dermis. Which of these layers is on the surface of the skin?

_____

2. Which layer is thicker, the epidermis or the dermis?

   _____

3. In which layer of the skin are blood vessels found?

   _____

4. The oil gland is attached to something that reaches the surface of the skin. What is it called?

   _____

5. The sweat gland connects to something that reaches the surface of the skin. What is it?

   _____

6. According to the passage, what happens when perspiration flows out of the skin?

   _____

7. How does the body stay warm in cold weather?

   _____

   _____

8. What is the main idea of the passage?

   _____

   _____

Check your answers on page 193.

Some bone fractures are easier to treat than others. Which of these fractures looks hardest to treat?

Study the diagram. Then answer the questions.

Bone Fractures

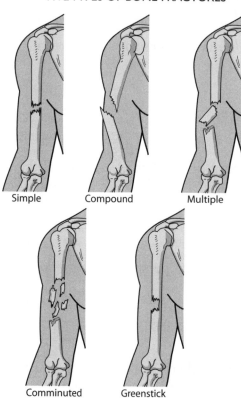

FIVE TYPES OF BONE FRACTURES

Simple   Compound   Multiple

Comminuted   Greenstick

1. In which type of fracture does the break go only partly through the bone?

_____

2. In which type of fracture does the bone break through the skin?

_____

3. In which type of fracture does the bone shatter into several small pieces?

_____

4. In which type of fracture does the bone break in more than one place?

_____

5. In which type of fracture is the bone broken all the way through in one place but the skin is

not torn? _____

Check your answers on page 193.

Try It Yourself!

In this chapter, you saw a diagram of human skin. The skin on the tip of your finger has a pattern of lines called a **fingerprint**. The skin on the palm of your hand has a pattern of lines too. It does not have as many lines as the fingertip. But the palm lines are deeper and clearer than the lines on the fingertip. Like fingerprints, there are probably no two palm prints alike. Try this experiment to compare palm prints.

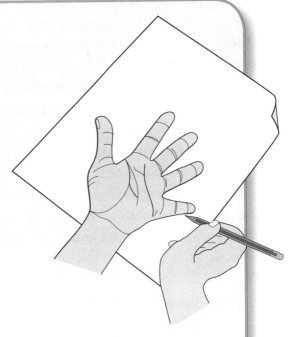

Materials you will need
a blank sheet of paper
a pencil

Steps
1. Take the hand that you do not write with. Lay it on the paper, palm up.
2. Trace around your hand to draw an outline of it on the paper. Then lift your hand from the paper.
3. Study the palm of that hand. On the outline that you made, draw in the main lines that you see. There should be four or five. Show where each line goes. Show if it goes all the way across your palm or only partway. Show if it splits in two.
4. Compare your palm drawing with the drawings or family members or friends. Does anyone else's look just like yours? Does anyone else's look almost like yours? Which lines are the most similar? Which lines are the most different?

UNIT 1

Review – Human Biology

Part A

Why do teeth get cavities? Why do some cavities cause pain while others do not?

Read the passage. Then answer the questions.

What Causes Tooth Decay?

Run your tongue across your teeth. Unless you have just brushed them, your teeth probably do not feel completely smooth and slippery. In fact, they probably have some sticky material on them. This material is called plaque. When you eat, tiny pieces of food remain in your mouth. Some pieces stick to your teeth. Then bacteria, a type of germ, begin growing on your teeth. This sticky mix of food and bacteria is plaque.

You can clean away most plaque by brushing your teeth and using dental floss. But the plaque that remains on a tooth can begin to eat into the tooth's surface. The result is a cavity, or tooth decay.

As long as the cavity remains near the surface of the tooth, it will not cause pain. But if the cavity keeps growing, it will reach the pulp of the tooth. This is where the nerves are. Once a cavity enters the pulp, the tooth will begin to ache.

1. What is plaque made up of? _____

2. Which sentence is the best summary of the first paragraph?
   (1) Plaque can make teeth feel rough instead of smooth and slippery.
   (2) Plaque can be cleaned away by brushing the teeth or using dental floss.
   (3) Plaque, a mixture of food and bacteria, sticks to the teeth and causes tooth decay.
   (4) Plaque is a sticky substance that gets on your teeth when you eat.

3. Number the following items in the order in which they occur:
   _____ Decay reaches the tooth's pulp.
   _____ The tooth hurts.
   _____ Tooth decay begins.
   _____ Plaque stays on the tooth.

Part B

Study the diagram. Then answer the questions.

THE TOOTH

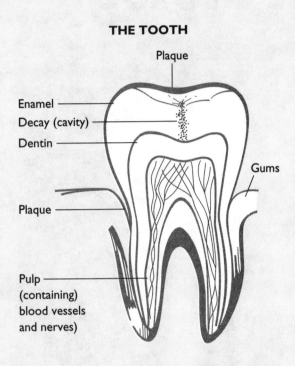

1. Which two parts of the tooth must a cavity grow through before it reaches the pulp?

   _____

2. What does pulp contain?

   _____

3. What layer has the cavity grown through in the diagram?

   _____

4. What parts of the tooth are above the gums?

   _____

Check your answers on page 193.

UNIT 2

Plant Biology

If all the living things on Earth were weighed, plants would make up about 99 percent of that weight. We depend on plants for the food that keeps us alive. All other animals do too. Without plants, all animals would die.

Plant biology is the study of plant life. Plant biologists study how plants fit in their environment and how we use plants as food.

Chapter	What You Will Learn About	What You Will Read
6	Restating Facts	The Food Chain Photosynthesis *and* Growing in Water Plant Defenses *and* Plant Medicine Cactus Plants *and* Useful Trees
7	Comparison and Contrast	Poison Ivy and Poison Oak The Giants of the Forest Plants That Live in Water Seeds *and* Plants, Animals, and Air
8	Classifying	Seeds *and* How Long Can Plants Live? Reproduction in Flowers Biomes Around the World Getting Along in a Tough Place
9	Drawing Conclusions	Food for the Soil Plants That Cheat Crazy for Catnip Big Trees, Little Shoots
10	Diagrams	Roots Leaves Classifying Trees That Tree Has a Ring Around It
Review	Plant Biology	Danger: Hungry Plant

After studying this unit, you should be able to

- restate ideas
- compare and contrast things and classify them into groups
- draw conclusions and understand diagrams

Restating Facts

When you understand an idea well, you can express the idea in a new way by using different words. This is called **restating**.

You probably restate ideas every day. For instance, imagine that you hear a weather forecast that says, "A thunderstorm will develop later in the day." When you make plans for the day, you might say, "It is supposed to rain this afternoon." That sentence restates the weather forecast. It uses different words, but the words mean the same thing.

When you learn something new, you can test how well you understand it by restating what you have learned in your own words. The words you use can be simpler than the original words. Think about this sentence: *Without plants, all animals on Earth would die out.* Can you restate this idea in your own words?

Begin by reading the sentence carefully. Be sure you understand it. Then look away from the sentence. Try to form a mental picture of the idea. Finally, use your own words to restate the idea in your mental picture. Write a sentence restating the idea.

_____

_____

There is more than one way to restate the sentence. Here are three examples of how the sentence could be restated.

All these sentences have the same meaning. They just use different words. A good restatement expresses the same idea as the original statement.

The Food Chain

Sentence	Restatement
Without plants, all animals on Earth would die out.	• All animals need plants to survive. • If it were not for plants, animals could not survive. • Animals cannot live without plants.

Match each statement on the left with its restatement on the right. On the line provided, write the letter of the correct restatement.

Sentence

_____ **1.** All animals depend on plants for their food.

_____ **2.** Not all animals eat plants.

_____ **3.** If an animal does not eat plants, it eats other animals that *do* eat plants.

Restatement

(a) Some animals eat only plant-eating animals.

(b) Without plants, animals would starve to death.

(c) Some animals do not eat plants.

Sentence 1 is restated in sentence (b).
Sentence 2 is restated in sentence (c).
Sentence 3 is restated in sentence (a).

Notice that the restatement sentences use different words, but they expresses the same meaning as the original sentence.

Restating information is a good way to check that you understand what you are reading.

Strategy: How to Restate Facts

- Read each statement carefully to be sure you understand it.
- Form a mental picture of the idea.
- Use your own words to express the same idea.

Exercise 1

PART A

Write the letter of the correct restatement on the line provided.

Photosynthesis

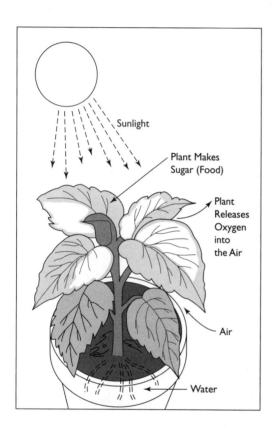

Sentence

_____ 1. Plants make their own food by a process called photosynthesis.

_____ 2. All a plant needs to make its own food is sunlight, water, and air.

_____ 3. With these natural "ingredients," a plant can produce sugars.

_____ 4. Later the plant can change the sugars into starch, protein, or fat.

_____ 5. These are exactly the same foods that humans need.

Restatement

(a) Once a plant has made sugars, it can change them into starch, protein, or fat.

(b) Photosynthesis is the name of the process used by plants to produce food.

(c) Plants make sugars out of these natural materials.

(d) Humans need the same kinds of food that plants make.

(e) With only sunlight, water, and air, a plant can make food.

Part B

Write the letter of the correct restatement on the line provided.

Growing in Water

Sentence	Restatement
_____ 1. Recently scientists discovered a new way to grow plants.	(a) In the future, hydroponics might be used in space colonies.
_____ 2. Instead of growing plants in soil, they grow plants on mats that hold water and plant **nutrients**.	(b) By using hydroponics, people can grow plants in layers so they will not need a lot of ground.
_____ 3. This system, called hydroponics, means plants can be grown in layers in tall buildings on only a small piece of ground.	(c) People can grow plants in spacecraft by using hydroponics.
	(d) There is a new way of growing plants.
_____ 4. Hydroponics will also be useful if people ever set up colonies in space.	(e) Plants do not need soil if they grow on a mat containing water and nutrients.
_____ 5. Even without soil, plants can be grown hydroponically in spacecraft.	

nutrients: substances that help growth or development

Circle the best answer to the question.

6. Which sentence best summarizes the sentences above?
   (1) Hydroponics is a way to grow plants on mats with water and nutrients.
   (2) Hydroponics is a new way to grow plants without soil, so plants can be grown in buildings and even in spacecraft.
   (3) Hydroponics is a new way to grow plants.
   (4) Hydroponics will one day be used in space colonies.

Check your answers on page 193.

Exercise 2

PART A

Write the letter of the correct restatement on the line provided.

Plant Defenses

Sentence

_____ 1. Some plants protect themselves from hungry animals with tiny needles that deliver a painful chemical when touched.

_____ 2. To discourage insects, the leaves of some plants are covered with a mat of fine hairs.

_____ 3. Other plants cover their leaves and stems with sharp thorns to keep animals away.

_____ 4. In a few plants, the leaves form cups that fill with water to drown insects that would like to eat them.

_____ 5. Some plants taste so terrible that no animal is willing to eat their leaves a second time.

Restatement

(a) The sharp thorns on other plants keep animals away.

(b) Sometimes rainwater forms pools in cups made by leaves, and insects drown in this water before they are able to eat the plant.

(c) Just touching some plants can cause pain. Being able to cause pain protects these plants from hungry animals.

(d) Some plants depend on the terrible taste of their leaves to protect them from being eaten by animals.

(e) A mat of fine hairs covers the leaves on some plants and makes it hard for hungry insects to eat the leaves.

Circle the best answer to the question.

6. Which sentence best summarizes the sentences above?
   (1) Plants use a variety of methods to protect themselves.
   (2) Touching the leaves of any plant is dangerous.
   (3) Most animals have discovered that eating plants can be painful.
   (4) Not every plant can protect itself from hungry animals.

PART B

Restate each sentence in your own words.

Plant Medicine

1. Plants are the source of many useful medicines.

   _____

2. The bark of the cinchona tree is the source of quinine, a medicine used to treat malaria.

   _____

3. The dried sap of a poppy gives us morphine, a powerful painkiller.

   _____

   _____

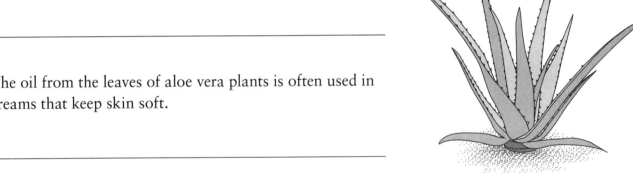

4. The oil from the leaves of aloe vera plants is often used in creams that keep skin soft.

   _____

   _____

Aloe Vera

Circle the best answer to the question.

5. Which sentence best summarizes the sentences above?
   (1) Many pain medicines are made from plants.
   (2) The best medicines are made from plants.
   (3) Medicines can be made from the bark, sap, and leaves of plants.
   (4) There would be no medicines if doctors did not use plants.

Check your answers on page 193.

Exercise 3

For Part A and Part B, restate each sentence in your own words.

Part A

Cactus Plants

1. Cactus plants have special features that help them survive with almost no water.

   _____

2. The cactus plant's wide stems can store large amounts of water.

   _____

   _____

3. Cactus stems have thick skins that keep the water inside them from drying up.

   _____

   _____

4. The cactus plant has very long roots that stay just below the surface of the sand.

   _____

5. Those roots quickly soak up any rain that falls.

   _____

Useful Trees

1. People use sap, the liquid in plant roots and stems, to make many substances.

   _____

2. The sap from the sapodilla, a Mexican jungle tree, is used in chewing gum.

   _____

3. Sap from sugar maple trees eventually becomes maple syrup, the topping used on pancakes.

   _____

Check your answers on page 194.

Try It Yourself!

The water in plants makes them firm and stiff. Test this with the following experiment.

Hypothesis
Plants become less firm as they lose water.

Test it!
Fill a glass with room temperature water. Cut off two stalks of celery with the leaves still on. Place the bottom of one stalk in the water. Do not put the second stalk in water. Place both stalks in sunlight. Check them in 15 minutes, in 30 minutes, in one hour, and in one day. Does one stalk get limp faster than the other? Which one? Why?

To extend this experiment, add food coloring to the water. What does this help you understand?

Record your observations. Write an explanation of why you think the plants changed as they did.

Check your results on page 194.

Chapter 7

Comparison and Contrast

When you study science, you will often find that two or more things are described at the same time. A writer may **compare** or **contrast** things. *Comparing* means "showing how things are alike." *Contrasting* means "showing how things are different."

You probably compare and contrast when you shop for groceries. Imagine you are in the supermarket buying orange juice. You see that orange juice comes in both cartons and bottles. After examining both of them, you say to yourself, "They both contain one-half gallon." That is comparing—noting how they are the same. Then you say, "But the bottle costs 30 cents more than the carton." That is contrasting—noting how they are different.

Here is a statement you might read in a science book: *Plants and animals are alike in that both can reproduce.* This sentence tells one way that plants and animals are the same. It is comparing plants and animals. The words *alike* and *both* are clues. They signal that the writer is talking about what is similar, or the same.

Now read this sentence: *Plants produce their own food, but animals cannot do this.* This sentence describes one way that plants and animals are different, so it is contrasting plants and animals. The word *but* is a clue. It signals the writer is describing a difference.

Read the following passage. It compares and contrasts two plants—poison ivy and poison oak.

Poison Ivy and Poison Oak

Would you recognize poison ivy and poison oak if you saw them? Both plants can cause severe skin irritation. Poison ivy plants usually have clusters of three leaves. The leaves are smooth, with smooth or saw-toothed edges. In late summer, white berries form on poison ivy plants.

Poison oak also has clusters of three leaves. These leaves are covered with fine hairs, and they have wavy edges. In late summer, poison oak develops yellow berries.

Did you notice the comparisons that the writer makes between poison ivy and poison oak? Here is one comparison: *Both can cause severe skin irritation.* The word *both* is a clue that the writer is describing a similarity, or sameness.

You should have noticed another comparison too. The first paragraph states *Poison ivy plants usually have clusters of three leaves.* Then the second paragraph states *Poison oak also has clusters of three leaves.* This similarity is not stated in the same sentence. You have to pay attention to notice it. The word *also* is a clue. It signals that the sentence refers to something mentioned earlier—something similar.

What contrasts did you find in this passage? Fill in the contrasts on the chart below. One difference has already been filled in.

CONTRASTS		
	Poison Ivy	**Poison Oak**
Leaves smooth or hairy?	Smooth	
Leaf edges		
Berry color		

If you completed the chart correctly, the poison ivy column should read, from top to bottom, *smooth, smooth or saw-toothed,* and *white*. The poison oak column should read, from top to bottom, *hairy, wavy,* and *yellow*.

Strategy: How to Find Comparisons and Contrasts

- Notice which features of the two (or more) things are being described.
- Look for clue words that signal similarities; for example, *both, all, like, alike, likewise, same, similar, also,* and *too.*
- Look for clue words that signal differences; for example, *but, however, unlike, different, although, on the other hand,* and *yet.*
- Make a chart showing the things that are described. List the features that are compared and the features that are contrasted.

Exercise 1

What is the tallest tree you have ever seen? Have you ever seen a tree that is as tall as a 30-story building?

Read the passage. Then, on the chart, put an X in the correct column for each statement.

The Giants of the Forest

If you visit a forest in California, you may see the giant of all trees—the sequoia (sih-KWOY-uh). Sequoias are among the largest and oldest living things on Earth.

One reason the sequoia lives so long is its bark. This tough bark grows to be twelve inches or more thick. It protects the tree against insects and diseases. The bark is almost fireproof. Thanks to their bark, most sequoias have survived at least one forest fire during their long lives.

The redwood tree is one type of sequoia. Redwoods grow near the Pacific coast in northern California and southern Oregon. They are the tallest trees in the world. Redwoods can grow as tall as a 30-story building. Of course, it takes several hundred years for them to reach this height. The tallest living tree in the world is a redwood. This tree is about 360 feet tall. It is 600 years old.

Another type of sequoia is the giant sequoia. It grows farther from the coast, in the Sierra Nevada of California. The giant sequoia does not grow quite as tall as the redwood. However, its trunk is thicker, so it actually contains more wood than the redwood. It also seems to live longer. Most giant sequoias cannot produce seeds until they are about 300 years old. Scientists believe that the oldest living sequoia is more than 3,000 years old.

THE GIANT SEQUOIA AT VARIOUS STAGES

500 years 1,000 years 2,000 years 3,000 years

250 feet
200 feet
150 feet
100 feet
50 feet

Source: *Monarchs of the Forest* by Annie Ensign Brown

	Redwood Tree	Giant Sequoia Tree	Both
1. It has tough, thick bark.			
2. The oldest living one is more than 3,000 years old.			
3. It grows near the Pacific coast in California and southern Oregon.			
4. It is likely to survive a forest fire.			
5. The tallest living one is about 360 feet tall.			
6. It contains the most wood.			
7. It has the thickest trunk.			
8. Its bark is almost fireproof.			

Check your answers on page 194.

Exercise 2

Plants that live on land have a hard time surviving when they get too much water. For some plants, however, there is no such thing as too much water.

Read the passage and complete the exercise.

LANGUAGE Tip

The word *aquatic* comes from the Latin word *aqua*, which means "water." The color aqua is greenish-blue.

Plants That Live in Water

When we think of plants, we usually think of plants that grow on dry land. However, ponds, lakes, streams, and rivers are home to a wide variety of plants. These plants are called **aquatic plants**. They have adapted to life in water or underwater.

If you visit a quiet pond, you might see a plant called a water-fern. Unlike most other plants, the water-fern floats freely in water. It gets the food it needs from the water, not from the soil. Its single root dangles in the water as the plant floats along with thousands of other water-ferns on the water's surface. One example of this kind of plant is the Mexican water-fern. It is found mostly in western North America and in northern South America. Its tiny leaves have two parts. The larger part floats on top of the water, and the smaller part stays underwater. The young plants are green, but older plants become pink or red. The Mexican water-fern has no flower, and it produces no fruit.

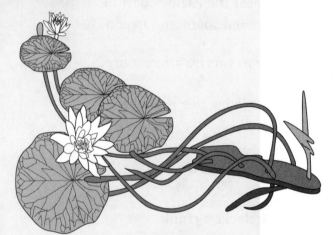

White Water Lily

The white water lily is, in many ways, different from the water-fern. This aquatic plant needs to be rooted in the soil. It grows best in ponds and shallow lakes that are three to six feet deep. Its roots cling to the mud at the bottom of the pond or lake. But its round leathery leaves float on top of the water. Each leaf is six to twelve inches wide. The leaves are green on the top side and purple on the underside. The white water lily has a large sweet-smelling flower, which blooms from June through October. The flower produces a fruit that contains seeds for new water lilies. The white water lily is native to eastern North America, but it grows well in other areas too.

Put an X in the correct column for each statement.

	Water-Fern	White Water Lily	Both
1. It can be found in the quiet water of ponds.			
2. Its flowers are large and fragrant.			
3. Its root floats freely in the water.			
4. It grows in North America.			
5. Its leaves have two parts, one underwater and one on the surface of the water.			
6. It has adapted to life in the water.			
7. It is rooted to the soil under the water.			
8. Its leaves are large, round, and leathery.			
9. It gets its food from the water itself.			
10. It produces a fruit.			
11. The underside of its leaves is purple.			
12. It turns from green to red.			
13. It is an aquatic plant.			

Check your answers on pages 194.

Exercise 3

Part A

Most plants make seeds that can grow into new plants. But how do seeds travel from their "parent" plants to a place where they can begin growing?

Read the passage. Then put an X in the correct column for each statement.

Seeds

One way that seeds travel is by "hitchhiking." Some hitchhiker seeds have tiny hairy hooks. These hooks can catch on the fur of a passing animal such as a raccoon. Later the seeds fall off the animal onto the groun. Then they may begin growing.

Other seeds are "fliers." These seeds are shaped like wings. When flier seeds fall from their parent plant, they can catch a breeze and float some distance before settling onto the ground.

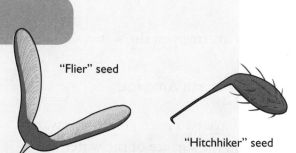

"Flier" seed

"Hitchhiker" seed

	"Hitchhiker" Seeds	"Flier" Seeds	Both
1. They are shaped like wings.			
2. They are carried by animals.			
3. They can move away from their parent plants.			
4. They have tiny hooks.			
5. Their design helps them travel.			
6. They are carried by air.			

Check your answers on page 194.

Part B

Read the passage. Then circle the best choice for each statment.

Plants, Animals, and Air

Plants and animals both need air to survive. Both "breathe in" the air in which they live. Animals use **oxygen**[1] from the air. Then they breathe out **carbon dioxide.**[2]

Plants are just the opposite. They use the carbon dioxide in the air to help make the food they need. Then, they "breathe out" the leftover oxygen through their leaves.

---

[1]**oxygen:** a gas that forms more than 20% of Earth's air
[2]**carbon dioxide:** a gas that forms less than 1% of Earth's air

1. They breathe in carbon dioxide.	Animals	Plants	Both
2. They need air to survive.	Animals	Plants	Both
3. They breathe out oxygen.	Animals	Plants	Both
4. They breathe in oxygen.	Animals	Plants	Both

Check your answers on page 194.

Try It Yourself!

In this chapter, you read that plants "breathe" through their leaves. Test this with the following experiment.

Hypothesis
Plants take in and give off gases through their leaves.

Test it!
Take a houseplant with many leaves. Gently smear a thick layer of petroleum jelly over both sides of two or three leaves. This will block the openings on the leaves. Watch the plant for about a week. Give it light and water as usual. What happens to the leaves coated with petroleum jelly? Why? Write down your observations.

Petroleum Jelly

Check your results on page 194.

Chapter 8

Classifying

Scientists often **classify** things, or sort them into groups. Everything in one group will have some feature in common. All things in another group will have a different feature in common.

Department stores classify their merchandise. Most department stores have signs naming the type of merchandise that is found in each area. Signs such as "Housewares," "Sporting Goods," and "Children's Clothing" help you find what you are looking for. If you need a certain item, you figure out which category the item fits into. Then you look for that part of the store. A toaster, for example, would most likely be in the category of housewares.

Study this example of classifying.

Seeds

Most plant seeds fall into one of two categories: naked or enclosed. As you might expect, naked seeds are uncovered. Plants that produce cones, such as pine trees, have naked seeds. The seeds rest on the scales of the cones.

Enclosed seeds are covered up. Flowering plants have enclosed seeds. Their seeds are enclosed in a part of the flower called the ovary. Fruits such as apples are actually the ovaries of flowering plants. Inside the ovaries are the seeds.

Did you notice the categories? They are *naked seeds* and *enclosed seeds*. When you read a passage that classifies, a chart can help you understand the information.

Categories	Naked Seeds	Enclosed Seeds
Features	I. Uncovered seeds 2. In plants with cones	I. Covered seeds 2. In flowering plants
Examples	pine trees	apple trees

Making a chart like this helps you remember the information. A chart can also be helpful if you want to classify other examples. For instance, suppose you want to know which type of seed a rose plant has. Looking back at the chart, you can see that flowering plants have enclosed seeds. Since roses are flowering plants, their seeds must be enclosed.

To practice classifying, read the following passage.

How Long Can Plants Live?

All plants can be classified into one of three groups.

An **annual** plant lives only one year. It flowers in the summer and then dies in the winter. Petunias are examples of annuals.

A **biennial** plant takes two years to complete its life. During the first summer, the plant grows leaves. In the winter, the plant rests and seems to dies. However, the next summer, it flowers, produces seeds, and finally dies. Forget-me-nots are biennials.

A **perennial** can live for many years. During the winter, it looks dead, but it is only resting. Peonies are perennials.

Now complete this chart, using the information in the passage.

Categories	Annuals	Biennials	Perennials
Feature	Live only one year		
Examples			

If you completed the chart correctly, the annual column should read (from top to bottom) *live only one year* and *petunias*. The biennial column should read (from top to bottom) *take two years to flower* and *forget-me-nots*. The perennial column should read (from top to bottom) *live many years* and *peonies*.

Now read this sentence: ***People who like begonias in their gardens must plant new ones every year.*** Look back at the chart. Can you figure out which category begonias belong to? The correct answer is ***annuals***, since annuals live for only one year.

Strategy: How to Classify

- Identify the categories.
- Note the features of each category.
- Put examples in their correct categories.

Exercise 1

You know that most plants produce young plants by making seeds. Did you know that many plants have both male and female parts?

Read the passage and complete the charts.

LANGUAGE Tip

Use this pronunciation guide as you read.

ovary	OH vah ree
style	STI el
pollen	PAH lin
stalk	STAWK
scent	SENT

Reproduction in Flowers

Most plants produce seeds in their flowers. One part of the flower is female. It is called the pistil. This part produces and stores eggs—just as female animals do. The diagram shows that the female part of the flower includes the ovary, the style, and the stigma.

The male part of the flower produces pollen. It is called the stamen. Before the plant can make seeds, the pollen must travel to the female part of the flower. There, the pollen joins with the eggs and **fertilizes** them. Only then can the eggs become seeds. The diagram shows that the male part includes the stalk and the anther.

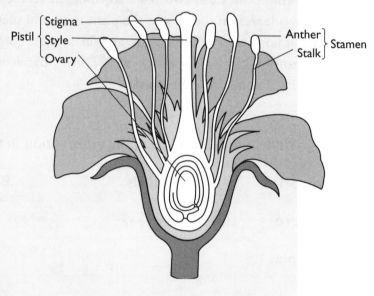

REPRODUCTIVE PARTS OF A FLOWER

How does pollen get from the stamen to the pistil of a flower? It usually travels in one of two ways. Wind can carry seeds. Wind-pollinated flowers are usually very small. They have no scent and no petals. Grass and most shade trees are wind-pollinated.

Insects can also carry pollen. Bees, yellow jackets, moths, and butterflies all get food from flowers. Pollen sticks to their legs and hair. Later, when the insect rubs against the pistil of the flower, pollen rubs off. Then the pollen fertilizes the flower.

Insect-pollinated flowers need to attract insects. Therefore, these flowers usually have a sweet scent and colorful petals. Examples of these flowers are orchids, wild roses, sunflowers, and daisies.

---

fertilizes: makes something able to develop and grow

Part A

Category	Female Flower Part	Male Flower Part
Name		
What It Produces		
Includes	1. 2. 3.	1. 2.

Part B

Category	Wind-Pollinated Flowers	Insect-Pollinated Flowers
Features	1. 2.	1. 2.
Examples	1. 2.	1. 2. 3. 4.

Check your answers on page 194.

Exercise 2

If you traveled around the world, you would see a wide variety of plants. Each type of plant is suited to live in the climate of the area where it grows.

Read the passage and complete the exercise.

LANGUAGE Tip

This passage compares and contrasts three climate areas. As you read, notice that each paragraph describes a new type of biome.

Biomes Around the World

The climate of an area determines the type of plant that will grow there. Consider, for example, deserts and rain forests. Rain rarely falls in a desert, but rain is almost always falling in a rain forest. If a plant needs plenty of water, it cannot grow in a desert. If it needs to dry out occasionally, it cannot survive in a rain forest. Around the world, there are various climate areas, or biomes. The plants that live in each biome perfectly match the climate in which they live.

Certain areas far north and far south of the equator are called tundra. In the tundra biome, the weather is cold and windy all year. Plants stay small there, to avoid being harmed by the strong, cold winds. Because the ground is frozen even in summer, tundra plants cannot send roots down deep into the soil. For that reason, they have shallow root systems. Some of the plants that grow in the tundra are grasses, mosses, and a few kinds of dwarf trees. One of those dwarf trees is the tiny arctic willow. It reaches a height of only about six inches.

The Mediterranean biome is quite different from the tundra biome. It is found around the Mediterranean Sea and in parts of California, South America, and Australia. The soil does not stay frozen there. In fact, the winters are warm and wet, and the summers are hot and dry. Plants can send deep roots down into the warm soil. Yet, because of the hot, dry summers, plants here tend to be short, usually less than three feet tall. Many of the shrubs and trees in the Mediterranean biome are evergreens. Some of these evergreens have needles. One such tree is the digger pine. Evergreens with leaves, such as the scrub oak, also thrive here.

Grassland biomes are usually located between forests and deserts. Grasslands can be found in Argentina, Australia, the center of the United States, and central and southern Africa. Rainfall in the grassland biome varies from about 10 to 30 inches per year. In areas where there is more rain, grasses grow tall, but the grasses are short where rainfall is limited. Trees grow near streams. Summers are very hot, and winters are very cold. Bush fires are common. Therefore, plants that grow in this biome must be hearty.

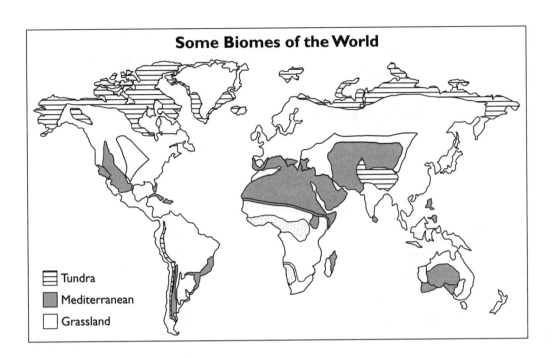

Some Biomes of the World

Tundra
Mediterranean
Grassland

Use the information in the passage to complete the chart.

Category	Tundra	Mediterranean Forest	Grassland
Location			
Weather			
Soil			
Plants that grow there	1. 2. 3.	1. 2.	1. 2.

Check your answers on page 195.

Exercise 3

Plants exist almost everywhere on Earth. However, plants differ greatly, depending on where they live. How do you think plants survive in a burning dry desert? How do they live in the dark waters of an ocean?

Read the passage and complete the chart.

Getting Along in a Tough Place

Different plants do very different things to survive in their natural homes. In the desert, for example, it seldom rains. When it does rain, desert plants store large amounts of rainwater in their stems. They use the water gradually during the long spells when no rain falls. Desert plants have thick skins. Their skins keep the stored water from **evaporating.** Cactuses are examples of this type of plant.

At the opposite extreme are plants that live in saltwater oceans. Most of these plants contain hollow spaces in which they store the air they must have to survive. Sargassum is one such plant. Kelp is another.

Because kelp has hollow spaces for air, it can live deep in the sea.

evaporating: changing from a liquid into a gas

Category		
Features	I. 2.	I.
Examples	I. cactus	I. sargassum 2. kelp

Check your answers on page 195.

Try It Yourself!

In this chapter, you have learned how the ovary of a flower produces seeds. The foods we call fruits are actually the ovaries of flowering plants. Each fruit contains one or more seeds.

Scientists define *vegetables* as "stems, leaves, and roots that can be eaten." Many of the foods that we call vegetables are actually fruits because they are the ovaries of flowering plants and they contain seeds.

List examples

Take paper and pencil to a supermarket. Make a list of the fruits and vegetables found in the produce department.

Classify them

When you get home, make a chart similar to the charts in this chapter. Write the categories *fruits* and *vegetables*. Then write short definitions of these terms.

For each item on your supermarket list, ask yourself, "Does this contain seeds?" If it does, it is probably a fruit. If you are not sure whether it contains seeds, ask someone. Classify and write each item under either *fruits* or *vegetables*.

How many things that we call "vegetables" do you think are actually fruits?

You may see some fruits that have no seeds, such as seedless grapes. You probably know that other grapes *do* have seeds. Scientists have simply learned how to make these plants produce fruits without seeds. If you like, you can make a third category on you chart. Use it for fruits without seeds. How many of these fruits can you find or think of?

Check your results on page 195.

Chapter 9

Drawing Conclusions

Writers do not always state all their ideas directly. Sometimes they only hint at their ideas. Then the reader must "read between the lines" to figure out what is being suggested. This process is called **drawing a conclusion.**

People draw conclusions all the time—sometimes the conclusions are correct, and sometimes they are not. Imagine that you work in a restaurant. One afternoon you notice many customers coming in carrying wet umbrellas.

You would probably conclude that it is raining. You might also conclude that rain is good for the restaurant business. If more people than usual are coming in to eat, that conclusion would be reasonable. Finally, you might conclude that a picnic planned for that evening will be canceled. This conclusion might turn out to be wrong. The sun may come out before evening, or the picnic may be held in an area with a shelter.

Here is a sentence you might read in a science book.

Scientists believe there are more than 350,000 kinds of plants in the world, but no one knows exactly how many.

What conclusions could you draw from this statement?

You might conclude that no one knows for sure because no one has ever recorded the names of all the kinds of plants. This is possible. But it does not seem likely. Scientists are usually very careful about recording information. This is probably not a good conclusion.

Another possible conclusion is that not all the plants in the world have been discovered. That seems more likely. There are areas of the world that have not been fully explored. Therefore, it is possible that some plants have not yet been discovered.

Study this short passage.

Food for the Soil

When the leaves of a tree fall in the autumn, they slowly rot and form a healthy "food" for the soil. The trees' roots hold the soil in place. They keep the soil from being washed away by rain or wind.

Below are three statements. Read each statement carefully. Then think about the facts in the passage. Which statements are logical conclusions?

(1) Fallen leaves should be raked away as soon as possible.
(2) Fallen leaves help the soil.
(3) Cutting down a tree can hurt the soil it grew in.

Statement (1) is not a good conclusion to draw from this passage. The passage describes how fallen leaves help the soil. The passage does not describe anything bad about fallen leaves. Quickly raking the leaves away does not make sense according to the facts presented here.

Statement (2) is a reasonable conclusion. It sums up the idea in the first sentence of the passage.

Statement (3) is also a good conclusion. It describes what would happen in the future if a tree were taken away. This statement is a good prediction based on the facts.

Strategy: How to Draw Conclusions

- Think of the facts as clues.
- Find ideas that the facts hint at but do not state directly.
- Be sure the ideas agree with the facts. Rule out ideas that do not make sense.

Exercise 1

You know that most plants use the energy of the sun to make their food. But just as some people try to take the easy way in life, some plants have found a way to avoid all the hard work of making food for themselves.

Read the passage and complete the exercise.

Plants That Cheat

Some plants cheat. They do not make their own food. Instead, they attach themselves to other plants and, in a way, steal food from them. We call these cheating plants "parasites."

Plants that are parasites usually do not have leaves or chlorophyll. Therefore, they cannot use energy from sunlight to make their own food. For that reason, they often live in dark, shadowy places. You may find them hidden under the roots or leaves of other plants.

Parasites do not put roots into the soil, as most plants do. Instead, they have suckers that attach themselves to the food channels in the stems and roots of larger plants. These larger plants are called hosts. Parasites use their suckers to pull from their hosts the water, sugars, and minerals that they need to survive.

Some plants are complete parasites; that is, in order to survive, they depend entirely on the host plant. If the host is healthy, they survive. If the host dies, however, they will die too unless they find a new host.

Other plants are partial parasites. They have their own green leaves, and they can use sunlight to make some food. However, they cannot make all the food they need. Mistletoe is an example of a partial parasite. There are about 200 kinds of bushes and trees that can be the host for mistletoe. In return for using its host, mistletoe helps the environment because many animals use its berries and leaves as food.

As you might expect, sometimes the host is harmed by the parasite. If the parasite becomes too large, it can drain too much water , sugars, and minerals from its host Parasites can destroy healthy trees and plants. They can kill whole fields of potato or tomato crops. In fact, each year farmers in the United States lose billions of dollars because of parasites.

Mistletoe

Write *yes* if the statement is a reasonable conclusion and *no* if it is not.

_____ 1. Plants that are parasites need water to grow.

_____ 2. A plant that is a partial parasite could live without a host.

_____ 3. Suckers work as well as roots for pulling in water.

_____ 4. A plant needs leaves and chlorophyll to produce its own food.

_____ 5. Mistletoe usually helps the tree or bush on which it grows.

Answer the questions in the space provided.

6. What makes mistletoe a partial parasite?

_____

7. How do parasites affect the income of farmers?

_____

8. In what way are parasites cheaters?

_____

9. Is it possible to have a field of parasites with no other plants around? Why or why not?

_____

10. How are parasites like other plants? How are they different?

_____

_____

Check your answers on page 195.

Exercise 2

Cats are usually calm. Hardly anything excites them. However, there is one substance that makes a well-mannered cat go crazy. Catnip!

Read the passage and complete the exercise.

LANGUAGE Tip

herb   ERB

In the United States, the *h* in *herb* is not pronounced. However, in England, the word is pronounced HERB.

Crazy for Catnip

The stuff seems quite ordinary to us. It does not have an interesting smell. Its dried leaves are an uninteresting greenish-gray color. It looks like any herb that you might add to a soup or a stew.

But sprinkle a little catnip near a cat, and watch the excitement. The cat will sniff, bat, and chew at the catnip. It will roll around in the catnip. It will meow. In general, the cat will act like it has gone crazy. However, this extreme reaction lasts for only a few minutes. Then the cat goes back to its normal behavior, at least for a few hours.

What is it in catnip that makes cats behave this way? Scientists tell us there is an oil on the plant's leaves that affects cats. The oil is released when the leaves are chewed, handled, or even brushed against. When the scent of the oil reaches organs in the cat's nose, the scent excites the cat.

Cats are not the only animals that enjoy catnip. The plant has been grown in European and American gardens for centuries. Some people believe that tea made from the leaves of catnip has a calming effect. Folk medicine says that catnip is useful for treating stomachaches and minor pains.

Recently scientists have discovered another fact about catnip oil. Insects hate it. In one experiment, the inside of one end of a glass tube was covered with catnip oil. Mosquitoes were put into the tube. All the mosquitoes tried to get as far away from the oil as possible. They crowded into the untreated end of the tube. In another experiment, scientists used two dead cockroaches. They covered one cockroach with catnip oil but not the other. Then they placed the cockroaches near ants. Normally ants would eat the dead cockroaches. Very soon the untreated cockroach was covered with ants. However, the cockroach covered with the catnip oil was left alone. Clearly, the ants wanted to have nothing to do with that cockroach because of the oil.

Who knows what scientists will learn in the future about the oil from this amazing plant?

Write *yes* if the statement is a reasonable conclusion and *no* if it is not.

_____ 1. Toys stuffed with catnip are popular gifts for cats.

_____ 2. Gardeners rarely plant catnip in home gardens.

_____ 3. Rubbing catnip oil on your body would probably keep insects from biting you.

_____ 4. It is hard to keep small insects away from catnip in the garden.

_____ 5. If you do not have a cat, there is no reason to plant catnip.

_____ 6. Scientists are interested in experimenting with catnip because they want to know more about it.

_____ 7. The smell of catnip usually makes humans feel sick.

Answer the questions in the space provided.

8. How do you think a cat would react to catnip after being away from it for a few hours?

_____

9. Could you successfully grow a catnip plant in a place where a cat could reach it? Why or why not?

_____

_____

10. If you placed a drop of catnip oil on the path between an ant and its food, what would the ant probably do?

_____

Check your answers on pages 195–196.

Exercise 3

You probably know that trees can grow from seeds. But do you know some other ways in which trees can reproduce?

Read the passage and complete the exercise.

Big Trees, Little Shoots

Most trees reproduce by bearing flowers. The flowers produce seeds that can grow into new plants. Some trees, however, can reproduce in other ways.

For instance, a birch tree that has been cut or blown down may sprout green shoots from its stump. These shoots can grow into new trees.

Apple trees produce flowers and seeds. But sometimes, green shoots also sprout from the tree roots. These shoots can develop into new trees.

Finally, a small twig cut from certain mature trees can be planted in the ground. The twig may develop roots and eventually become a tree.

Write *yes* if the statement is a reasonable conclusion. Write *no* if it is not.

_____ 1. All trees can reproduce in several different ways.

_____ 2. Most trees make seeds.

_____ 3. If you cut a twig from a mature tree, the tree is likely to die.

_____ 4. Most apple trees grow from seeds.

Answer the questions in the space provided.

5. How do most trees reproduce? _____

6. How can apple trees reproduce? _____

7. What is one similarity between birch trees and apple trees, according to the passage?

_____

Check your answers on page 196.

Try It Yourself!

In this chapter, you have learned about seeds sprouting into plants. This experiment will help you learn about what makes a seed sprout.

Materials you will need
15 kernels of unpopped popcorn
(or other seeds)
3 paper towels
3 plastic sandwich bags
very hot water

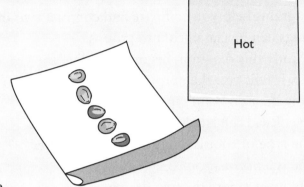

Steps

1. Boil ½ cup of water. Soak 5 seeds in the hot water for 15 minutes.
2. In a ½ cup of room-temperature water, soak 10 seeds for 15 minutes.
3. Label the three sandwich bags: hot, cold, room temperature.
4. Moisten 3 paper towels. On one paper towel, spread out the 5 seeds that were boiled. Place 5 of the room-temperature seeds on each of the other two paper towels. Then roll up the paper towels.
5. Place the paper towel containing the 5 seeds that soaked in boiling water into the bag labeled "hot." Set this bag in a sunny window or another very warm place.
6. Place the second paper towel in the bag labeled "cold." Set this bag in the refrigerator.
7. Place the last paper towel in the bag labeled "room temperature." Set this bag where it does not receive direct sunlight.
8. Keep the paper towels moist for the next five days.

Observe
Which seeds sprout faster? Do all the seeds sprout?

Draw Conclusions
Draw a conclusion about what helps seeds sprout. What does this experiment help you understand about the growth of plants? Write down your conclusions.

Check your results on page 196.

Chapter 10

Diagrams

Diagrams are important in science. They let readers see what is being described. Diagrams help you compare and contrast two or more things. They can also show how things can be classified into groups.

Study this diagram. Begin by reading the title. It tells you the purpose of the diagram—to show the two main types of roots that plants have. Read the labels beneath the drawings. One type of root is a *taproot*, and the other type is a *fibrous root*.

Now compare the two drawings. What similarities do you see? Both plants have roots anchored in the soil. Both have many thin, hair-like roots that reach in different directions into the soil.

You can also contrast the drawings by noting differences. The fibrous root plant has more hair-like roots than the plant with the taproot. All the fibrous roots are about the same size. By contrast, the plant with the taproot has one root in the middle that is longer and thicker than the other roots. (That middle root is the taproot.)

A chart showing these similarities and differences would look like this.

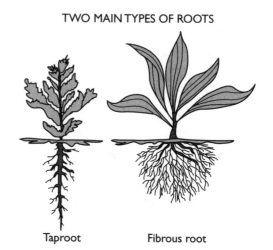

TWO MAIN TYPES OF ROOTS

Taproot   Fibrous root

Roots

Root Types	Taproot	Fibrous Root
Similarities	1. Roots are anchored in the soil. 2. Many hair-like roots reach in different directions into the soil.	
Differences	1. Fewer hair-like roots 2. Root in the middle is longer and thicker	1. More hair-like roots 2. All roots about the same size.

Now suppose you were asked to classify carrots and grass as having either taproots or fibrous roots. Study the following diagram of the two plants.

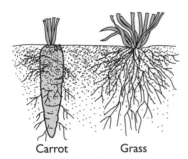

Carrot   Grass

How would you classify the carrot? Compare this diagram to the diagram on the previous page. The carrot has a taproot—one root in the middle that is longer and thicker than the other roots. In fact, the taproot is the part of the carrot plant that people eat. The grass plant has a fibrous root. Grass has many hair-like roots that are all the same size.

Now study the next diagram. Answer the questions that follow.

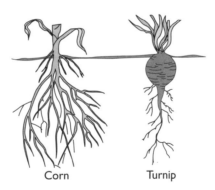

Corn   Turnip

What type of root does corn have? _____
If you wrote *fibrous root*, you were right.

What type of root does the turnip have? _____
If you wrote *taproot*, you were right.

Strategy: **How to Read Diagrams**

- Read the title to learn the purpose of the diagram.
- Study the drawings and the labels.
- If there are two or more drawings, compare and contrast them.

Study the diagram and answer the questions.

Leaves

LEAF EDGES IN BROADLEAF PLANTS

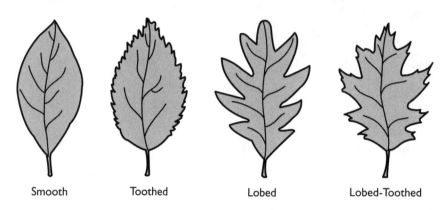

Smooth   Toothed   Lobed   Lobed-Toothed

1. How are smooth leaves different from the other three types of leaves?

   _____

2. How are toothed leaves different from the other three types of leaves?

   _____

3. How are lobed leaves different from the other three types of leaves?

   _____

4. How are lobed-toothed leaves different from the other three types of leaves?

   _____

Check your answers on page 196.

Exercise 2

Study the diagram below. Then look back at the diagram on the previous page. Use that diagram to classify these trees according to their leaf edges.

LANGUAGE *Tip*

The leaves on an evergreen tree are frequently called "needles" because of their shape. Evergreen trees keep their leaves for several years.

Classifying Trees

FOUR COMMON U. S. CITY TREES

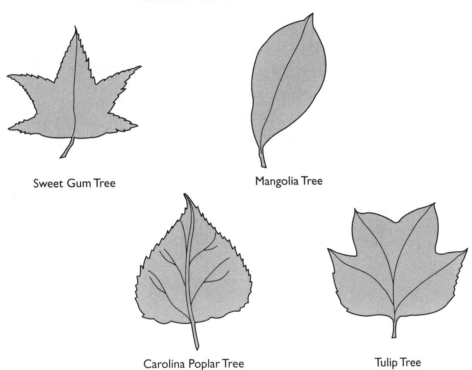

Sweet Gum Tree

Mangolia Tree

Carolina Poplar Tree

Tulip Tree

1. Sweet gum tree _____

2. Magnolia tree _____

3. Carolina poplar tree _____

4. Tulip tree _____

Check your answers on page 196.

How can you tell the age of a tree?

Read the passage and study the diagram. Then circle the best answer to each question.

That Tree Has a Ring Around It

Trees and shrubs are supported by a woody stem, or a trunk. Each year a tree lives, the stem gets thicker. The year's growth can usually be seen in a layer of the wood called a growth ring. This ring forms a circle around the stem.

The outer layer of a tree stem is called the bark. Bark moves food to the various parts of the tree. Water moves through an inner layer of the stem called the sapwood. The layer at the center of the stem is called heartwood. This layer is old wood that no longer carries water.

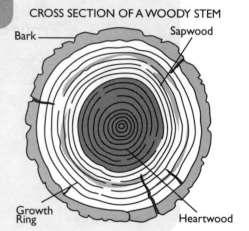

CROSS SECTION OF A WOODY STEM

Bark — Sapwood

Growth Ring — Heartwood

1. About how old is the tree in the diagram?
   (1) 5 years
   (2) 9 years
   (3) 20 years
   (4) 42 years

2. Where is sapwood found?
   (1) at the center of the stem
   (2) on the tree branches only
   (3) on the outside of the stem
   (4) between the bark and the heartwood

3. Bark transports food to various part of the tree. According to this information, which is a reasonable conclusion?
   (1) Trees need bark to live.
   (2) Trees can survive without bark.
   (3) Trees need bark only in the winter.
   (4) Trees need bark only in the summer.

Check your answers on page 196.

Try It Yourself!

This chapter explains how diagrams can help you compare and contrast or classify different things. In this project, you will make your own diagrams.

Collect one leaf from four or five different plants or trees in your neighborhood. Be sure they are broad leaves, not the narrow, pointed needles of evergreens. Put each leaf in a separate envelope. On the envelope, write where you found the plant.

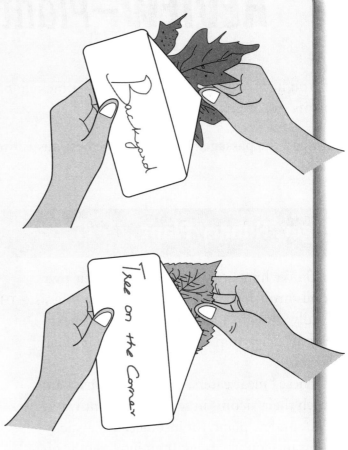

As soon as possible, make a drawing of each leaf. You can trace the outline if this is easier. Do not wait too long to do this. Leaves curl up and become stiff after they are picked. Below each drawing, write where you found the plant.

Use the diagram on page 82 to identify the type of leaf edge on each of your leaves. Write the name of the type below the plant's location. When you are finished, you will have a diagram of leaf types found in your neighborhood.

UNIT 2

REVIEW—Plant Biology

You have probably heard of insects attacking plants. But do you know that some plants can attack insects?

Read the passage. Then circle the best answer to each question.

Danger: Hungry Plant

Unlike humans, all plants make their own food through a process called photosynthesis. Oddly enough, a few plants are also "meat eaters." They trap and digest insects in their leaves.

THE HINGED LEAF OF THE VENUS FLYTRAP

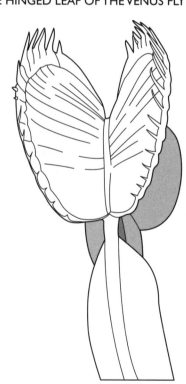

These "meat eaters," or carnivorous plants, catch their victims in several different ways. The sundew plant, for instance, has a sticky substance on its leaves. If an insect lands on that substance, the insect becomes stuck and cannot escape. The plant's tentacles surround the insect. They help the plant **digest** the insect.

A famous member of the sundew family is the Venus flytrap. This carnivorous plant has hinged leaves. The leaves snap shut around any insect that strays too close. The plant digests an insect in about ten days.

Scientists have found about 3,000 carnivorous plants. This is only a very small number of the world's plants. In spite of their strange habits, these plants also make food through photosynthesis, just as common plants do.

---

digest: convert food into simple forms that the body can use

1. Which is a good restatement of the description of the Venus flytrap given in the passage?
   (1) When an insect comes near the Venus flytrap, the plant catches it like a trap.
   (2) When an insect flies near the Venus flytrap, it can get caught on the plant's sticky leaves.
   (3) Insects sometimes snap their mouths shut on a leaf of a Venus flytrap.
   (4) The Venus flytrap moves its leaves toward an insect to trap the insect.

2. Carnivorous plants use certain animals as food. In this way, they are like
   (1) all other plants
   (2) humans who eat meat
   (3) humans who eat meat and other plants
   (4) people who do not eat meat

3. Which of the following make food through the process of photosynthesis?
   (1) only carnivorous plants
   (2) all plants except carnivorous plants
   (3) carnivorous plants and other plants
   (4) carnivorous plants and humans

4. The term *carnivorous* means
   (1) hungry
   (2) meat-eating
   (3) unusual
   (4) Venus flytrap

5. A plant called Venus's looking glass has purple or blue flowers. The plant gets food only through photosynthesis. Is Venus's looking glass a carnivorous plant?
   (1) yes
   (2) no

6. According to the facts in the passage, is this statement a reasonable conclusion? *Some carnivorous plants move in unusual ways to catch their victims.*
   (1) yes
   (2) no

Check your answers on page 196.

UNIT 3

Physics

Why do things fall down instead of drift up or float? What makes a rolling ball slow down and stop? How can one thing make another thing warm? These are some of the questions answered by a branch of science called **physics.**

Physics is the study of matter, energy, and force. More specifically, physics explores such topics as light, sound, heat, air, and motion.

Chapter	What You Will Learn About	What You Will Read
11	Identifying Facts and Opinions	Energy, Old and New Shining Light on an Old Problem Block That Inertia! On Slippery Ice
12	Making a Hypothesis	What Is Happening on Mars? Figuring Out What Is Happening What Went Wrong? Explaining What You See
13	The Scientific Method	Staying Warm: Wool or Cotton? Sounds Strange to Me What Makes Some "Cold" Things Cold? Exploring the Moon
Review	Physics	Is There Such a Thing as White Light?

After studying this unit, you should be able to

- identify facts and opinions

- make scientific hypotheses

- define the steps in the scientific method

Chapter 11

Identifying Facts and Opinions

Scientists try to explain the world around us. They try to understand what things are made of and how they work.

When you study science, you learn facts that scientists have discovered about the natural world. But sometimes you also read a writer's opinion. It is important to be able to tell whether a statement is a fact or an opinion.

A **fact** is a statement that can be proved. Here is an example: *At 2:30 this afternoon, there was a brief rainstorm.* How could this statement be proved? People may have seen the rainstorm. They may have felt the rain if they went outside. Someone may have recorded the storm on film. All of this information is **evidence**, or proof, that it rained. With evidence like this, reasonable people would agree that the statement is a fact.

Here is another statement: *The rainstorm was a welcome relief from the summer heat.* Is this a fact too? No, it is an **opinion**—a statement that cannot be proved. An opinion is a statement expressing a personal belief or preference. Not everyone agrees with an opinion. People who like heat and hate rain would not agree with the statement. An opinion cannot be proved with evidence. Even if the statement is a reasonable opinion, it is still an opinion. It is not a fact.

Study the following sentences. Which sentences are facts?

(1) **Sound is caused by air vibrating, or moving back and forth.**
(2) **Very loud sounds can permanently damage a person's ears.**
(3) **People working in noisy factories should wear earplugs.**

Sentence (1) is a fact. It can be proved with evidence from a machine called an oscilloscope. This machine makes pictures of the vibrations that cause sound. Scientists have also proved the truth of sentence (2). They have examined the effects of loud sounds on people's ears.

Sentence (3), however, is *not* a fact. It is an opinion. Notice the word *should*. It is a clue that the statement gives the writer's opinion about how something *ought to be*. It may be a reasonable opinion. Most people may agree with the opinion. But the statement is still an opinion. It is not a fact that can be proved.

Identify the facts and opinions in the following passage.

Energy, Old and New

(1) Scientists define *energy* as "the ability to do work." (2) Hundreds of years ago, people used animals and natural forces such as wind and rivers to help them do work. (3) Then new sources of energy were discovered, including steam power, electrical power, and nuclear power. (4) Today we should think carefully about the energy we use. (5) We must be sure that we do not pollute our environment by using energy.

Which of the sentences are facts—statements that can be proved? Sentence (1) can be proved by checking a dictionary. Sentence (2) can be proved by looking at drawings made long ago or by reading history books. They will describe people using animals, windmills, or water mills to help them do work. Sentence (3) can also be proved with evidence from history.

Sentence (4) is the first opinion in the passage. It cannot be proved with evidence. The sentence states the writer's belief about what is important. The word *should* is a clue that this sentence states an opinion.

Did you figure out what sentence (5) is? It is an opinion. The word *must* is a clue. *Must* is another way of saying "should."

Strategy: How to Identify Facts and Opinions

- Think about whether the statement can be proved with evidence.
- Think about whether everyone would agree with the statement after seeing the evidence.
- Look for words that signal opinions, such as *should* or *should not, must* or *must not,* or *ought to.*
- Look for words expressing emotions or values. These words often signal opinions. Examples include *good, bad, best, great, important, beautiful, terrible, wonderful,* or *fun.*

Exercise 1

The Sun can help us save money and cut down on pollution. Can you guess how?

Read the passage and complete the exercise.

LANGUAGE Tip

Solar panels are expensive. The governments of Japan and several European countries are helping citizens buy solar panels in order to help protect the environment.

Shining Light on an Old Problem

(1) Americans ought to take more advantage of the Sun's energy. (2) Sunlight doesn't cost anything, and it doesn't pollute the environment.

(3) Some people have already turned to the Sun to heat their homes. (4) First, sunlight heats water inside a dark panel. (5) Then pipes carry the hot water through the home to heat the air. (6) Heating by sunlight is much better than heating by gas, oil, or electricity.

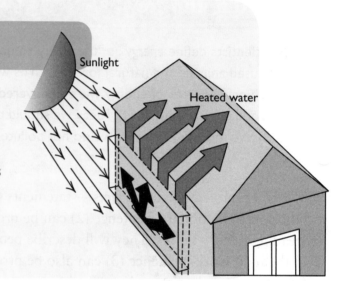

Sunlight

Heated water

Write *F* if the sentence above is a fact. Write *O* if it is an opinion.

1. sentence (1) _____

2. sentence (2) _____

3. sentence (3) _____

4. sentence (4) _____

5. sentence (5) _____

6. sentence (6) _____

Check your answers on page 196.

Exercise 2

You probably know why cars have seat belts. But do you know which law of physics makes seat belts necessary?

Read the passage and answer the questions.

Block That Inertia!

(1) Seat belts are the most important change that has been made to cars in the past 50 year. (2) Seat belts were designed to protect people from being hurt in automobile accidents.

(3) A physical force called inertia is the reason why car accidents can be so dangerous. (4) Drivers—and passengers too—need to understand inertia. (5) Because of inertia, an object at rest will not move unless it is forced to move. (6) Also because of inertia, a moving object will keep moving unless something stops it.

(7) If you are inside a moving car, you are moving in the same direction as the car. (8) If the car stops suddenly, inertia will make you keep moving in the same direction. (9) You will continue to move in that direction until something slows you down or stops you. (10) If you are in the front seat without a seat belt on, the "something" that stops you may be the windshield. (11) Clearly, it is foolish not to wear a seat belt.

1. Which sentence in the first paragraph is an opinion? _____

2. Which sentence in the second paragraph is an opinion? _____

3. Which sentence in the third paragraph is an opinion? _____

Check your answers on page 196.

Exercise 3

Like other athletes, ice skaters have to work against several forces of physics. How can skaters improve their chances against one of these forces?

Read the passage and complete the exercise.

On Slippery Ice

(1) Ice skating is a lot of fun. (2) It is the most fun when the ice is smooth and the blades of the skates are sharp. (3) With smooth ice and sharp blades, you will feel the least friction when you skate.

(4) Friction is a force that occurs when two objects rub against each other. (5) Friction slows down moving objects and keeps still objects from moving. (6) Objects with smooth surfaces produce less friction when rubbed together than objects with rough or bumpy surfaces.

(7) When you glide across the ice on skates, the surface of your skate blades rubs against the surface of the ice. (8) Smooth ice reduces friction. (9) With less friction, you can glide faster and farther. (10) Rusty or scratched blades increase friction, and this friction will slow you down. (11) To make the least friction, you need very smooth ice *and* very sharp skate blades. (12) For this reason, skaters should always protect their blades when they are off the ice.

Write *F* if the sentence above is a fact. Write *O* if it is an opinion.

1. sentence (1) _____
2. sentence (2) _____
3. sentence (3) _____
4. sentence (4) _____
5. sentence (5) _____
6. sentence (6) _____

7. sentence (7) _____
8. sentence (8) _____
9. sentence (9) _____
10. sentence (10) _____
11. sentence (11) _____
12. sentence (12) _____

Check your answers on page 196.

Try It Yourself!

In this chapter, you have learned about friction. Do this experiment to learn more about friction.

Materials you will need

a long, flat board that can be used as
    a ramp (You can make a table into
    a ramp by putting books under
    two of the table legs.)
toy cars
yardstick
various coverings for the ramp
    (such as a towel, a piece of plastic,
    wood, cardboard, aluminum foil)

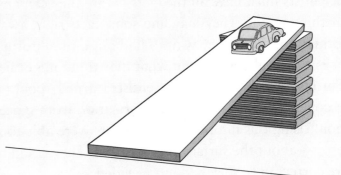

Steps

1. Use the board to create a ramp. Hold a toy car at one end of the ramp.
2. Let go of the car, but do not push it. Measure how far the car moves down the ramp. Record your findings.
3. Change the surface of the board and repeat the experiment. Use rough materials and smooth materials.
4. Change the weight of the toy car by using a bigger or smaller toy car.

Draw Your Conclusions

Which surface creates the most friction? Do light-weight or heavy-weight objects create the most friction? Write your conclusions, and explain why you drew these conclusions.

Check your results on page 197.

Chapter 12

Making a Hypothesis

Scientists must have all the facts before they can answer questions or prove that something is true. They may find some facts right away. Then they must search for more information. While they wait to find out more information, they develop a **hypothesis**. This is a careful guess about what they think might be true.

For instance, before 1969 scientists learned about the Moon by studying it through telescopes. They also gathered information from space flights that passed close to the Moon. Using this information, scientists were able to make hypotheses—educated guesses—about the surface of the Moon. They could not test whether their hypotheses were correct until they had more evidence.

Astronauts finally landed on the Moon in 1969. They brought back samples of Moon rocks. Scientists now had the evidence they needed. They could test whether their hypotheses about the Moon's surface had been correct.

A hypothesis is an educated guess meant to explain facts. A hypothesis has not yet been proved. Hypotheses can be proved or disproved in the future once more evidence has been found. Notice that a hypothesis is not the same as an opinion. An opinion can never be proved or disproved. A hypothesis *can* be proved when there is more information.

We all make hypotheses every day. Imagine, for example, that a friend of yours works at a store that is going out of business soon—but you do not know exactly when. One day you call your friend at work. No one answers the phone. You might make the hypothesis that the store has finally gone out of business. That is a reasonable guess. But you will not know if your hypothesis is true until you find more information.

Study the following example of hypotheses in science.

What Is Happening on Mars?

For many years, scientists studied the planet Mars through powerful telescopes. They saw that the marks on the surface of the planet did not always look the same. Scientists wondered what caused the marks to change.

In 1976, the American spacecraft *Viking I* landed on Mars. It picked up samples of the dust that covered much of the planet. It also recorded very strong winds that blew much of the time. Those winds caused dust storms that swirled around the *Viking I* spacecraft.

In early 2004, two Mars Exploration Rovers, *Spirit* and *Opportunity,* landed on Mars. They traveled over the planet, testing rocks and exploring the surface of Mars. They survived month-long severe dust storms and temperatures of −35° Fahrenheit.

With the help of the facts gathered by these rovers, scientists formed new ideas about Mars. They now believe that the changes in the marks on the planet's surface may be a result of the dust storms. Scientists are still learning more about Mars. Perhaps one day they will know if their idea is correct.

The passage begins by describing the question scientists asked: *What causes the marks on the surface of Mars to change?* Next, you read about the facts discovered when *Viking I, Spirit, and Opportunity* landed on Mars. One important fact is that Mars has dust on its surface. Another fact is that Mars has strong winds and severe dust storms.

Once scientists knew these facts, they formed a hypothesis. Did you notice the hypothesis? *They [scientists] now believe that the changes in the marks on the planet's surface may be a result of the dust storms.* The words *believe* and *may be* are clues that signal a hypothesis.

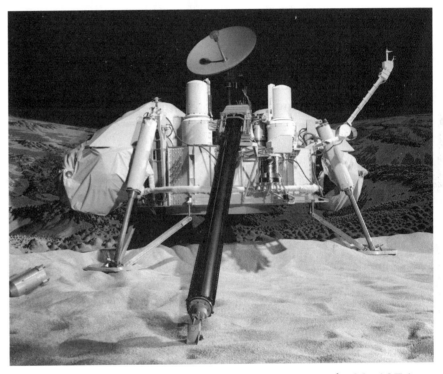

Viking I Lander touched down on Mars on July 20, 1976.

Strategy: How to Recognize a Hypothesis

- Identify the question being asked.
- Look for words such as *think, may be, might be, possibly,* and *probably*. These words may signal an educated guess.
- Ask yourself if the educated guess answers the question being asked.
- Look for evidence that supports the educated guess.

Exercise 1

Read each passage. Then circle the hypothesis that best explains the facts.

Figuring Out What Is Happening

To experiment with friction, Juanita rubbed the palms of her hands together for one minute. As she did this, she noticed that her hands got warmer and warmer.

1. She made the hypothesis that
   (1) her hands were cold when she began the experiment
   (2) the experiment increased the temperature in the room
   (3) friction produces heat
   (4) the longer friction continues, the stronger the friction becomes

After her palms had cooled off, Juanita shook some talcum powder onto them. Then she rubbed them together again for one minute. This time, they did not become as warm as they had the first time.

2. She made the hypothesis that
   (1) talcum powder reduces the friction between two objects
   (2) the talcum powder was cold
   (3) talcum powder never becomes warm
   (4) the talcum powder dissolved in her hands

On a hot summer day, Nan decided to measure the temperature in her living room. She held a thermometer in several different places. The thermometer showed that the air near the ceiling was warmer than the air near the floor.

3. Nan made the hypothesis that
   (1) thermometers cannot show the same temperature for any length of time
   (2) it was warmer indoors than outdoors
   (3) warmer air rises above cooler air
   (4) warm air is heavier than cool air

The next winter, Nan turned on the heat in her house. The air was soon warmer near the ceiling than near the floor. She then turned on a ceiling fan. Soon the air was just about the same temperature near the ceiling and near the floor.

4. Nan made the hypothesis that
   (1) warm air and cool air mix evenly in the winter
   (2) the ceiling fan was pushing warm air toward the floor
   (3) the ceiling fan did not affect the air
   (4) the air temperature is the same in all areas of the house

Which takes more force—lifting an object straight up or pushing an object up a smooth slope?

Lucy was moving into an apartment building with six steps at the front entrance. She needed to carry in a suitcase, but the suitcase was too heavy. She could not lift it. Then a neighbor put the suitcase on a ramp next to the steps. Lucy tried again to lift the suitcase. It would not move, but she could move it if she pushed it up the ramp.

5. Lucy hypothesized that
   (1) it was a shorter distance to go up the ramp than up the steps
   (2) it takes less force to push an object up a smooth slope than it does to lift it straight up
   (3) an object is heavier when it is resting on the ground than when it is resting on a ramp
   (4) an object weighs less when it is slanted than when it is standing straight up

Check your answers on page 197.

Exercise 2

Read each paragraph and complete the exercises.

LANGUAGE Tip

Irregular Verbs

The past tense of the verb *lie* is *lay*.

Present tense: Now the sandwiches **lie** in water.

Past tense: Yesterday the sandwiches **lay** in water.

What Went Wrong?

(1) On a hot summer day, Calvin and Rose went to the lake shore. (2) Rose packed a cooler with everything needed for a picnic dinner. (3) Calvin carried the cooler to the car and put it into the trunk. (4) Because of road work, the drive to the beach took longer than usual. (5) All traffic came to a stop several times, and Calvin turned off the air conditioner to save gas. (6) Finally they arrived at the beach. (7) Calvin carried the cooler to a picnic table and opened it. (8) Inside, the cans of soda were standing in several inches of water. (9) Sandwiches in plastic bags lay floating on top of the water.

1. When Calvin saw what was in the cooler, he made a hypothesis about what Rose had packed. What did Calvin think Rose had put into the cooler?
   (1) sandwiches in plastic bags, cans of soda, and water
   (2) water, sandwiches, cans of soda, and empty plastic bags
   (3) sandwiches in plastic bags, cans of soda, and loose ice cubes
   (4) ice cubes in plastic bags, cans of soda, and sandwiches

2. Calvin made another hypothesis about what had happened to the cooler and its contents. Which sentence states his hypothesis?
   (1) When the car was stopped in traffic, vandals broke into the trunk and poured water into the cooler.
   (2) The trunk of the car got so hot that the ice in the cooler melted.
   (3) The sandwiches were hot when Rose packed them, so they melted the ice.
   (4) The items in the cooler were exactly as Rose had packed them.

3. Which sentence from the paragraph does NOT provide support for Calvin's hypothesis?
   (1) sentence (1)
   (2) sentence (4)
   (3) sentence (5)
   (4) sentence (7)

Calvin and Rose stayed on the beach until dark. As night fell, Calvin went back to the car for his flashlight. Returning to the beach, he dropped the flashlight in the sand. When he picked it up, it would not turn on again.

"What is wrong with your flashlight?" Rose asked.

"I am not sure, but I have some ideas," Calvin answered.

4. Calvin took apart the flashlight, wiped off each part, and put the parts back together. What did he think was wrong?
   (1) The bulb had broken in the fall.
   (2) The flow of electricity from the battery was blocked by water that entered the flashlight while he was carrying it toward the lake.
   (3) The flow of electricity from the battery was blocked by sand that entered the flashlight when it fell to the ground.
   (4) The flashlight had not been put together correctly when he bought it.

5. Later Calvin put a new battery into the flashlight. What was he thinking was wrong?
   (1) The bulb had broken in the fall.
   (2) The battery had run out of power.
   (3) The flow of electricity from the battery was blocked by sand.
   (4) The flashlight had not been put together been correctly.

Check your answers on page 197.

Exercise 3

Read each passage and write a scientific hypothesis to explain the set of facts. Then underline the evidence in the passage that led to that hypothesis.

Explaining What You See

Tony got a new laptop for his birthday. He put it on his desk, which he shared with his brother Cal. Tony went out for a while that evening. He made Cal promise not to use the new laptop. Tony came back an hour later. He felt the top of the laptop. It was warm.

1. What was Tony's hypothesis about why the laptop was warm?

_____

Cal said he had not been using the new laptop. He had made some hot chocolate and had done his homework. He said he had put the cup of hot chocolate on top of the laptop. He had taken the cup to the kitchen just before Tony walked in. Tony thought Cal looked as if he was telling the truth.

2. What was his hypothesis now about why the laptop was warm?

_____

On the kitchen table, Tony saw Cal's cup, still half-full of hot chocolate. It was an insulated cup. An insulated cup keeps a drink hot, but the cup itself stays cool.

3. What was Tony's hypothesis now?

_____

Near Dave's farm, there are above-ground telephone poles strung with wires. Usually the wires hang tightly, sagging very little between the poles. One sunny afternoon in the summer, Dave noticed that the telephone wires were sagging more than usual. He knows that most things expand, or get bigger, when they are heated.

4. What hypothesis did he make to explain what he saw?

_____

Teresa and Mona drove to a campground high in the mountains. A week later, they drove home on the same route. They kept track of how much gas the car used on both parts of the trip. They found that the car used more gas on the trip to the campground. Teresa and Mona know that gravity pulls things down toward Earth.

5. What hypothesis did they make to explain why the car used more gas on the first trip?

_____

_____

Check your answers on page 197.

Try It Yourself!

In this chapter, you have learned that heat makes things expand, or get larger. Try this experiment to learn about hot and cold air.

Hypothesis
Heat makes things expand, and cold makes things contract (get smaller).

Materials you will need
a plastic bottle
small balloon
boiling water in a pan
ice water in a large bowl

Steps
1. Fill the bottle about one-fourth full of water.
2. Place the balloon over the mouth of the bottle.
3. Set the bottle into a pan of very hot water. Then watch what happens.
4. Place the bottle (with the balloon on it) into the ice water. Then watch what happens.

Describe what you observed and why you think things happened as they did.

Check your results on pages 197–198.

Chapter 13

The Scientific Method

Detectives solve mysteries by collecting evidence and looking for clues. Scientists are like detectives. They try to unlock the mysteries of science by using the **scientific method**. The scientific method is a step-by-step process for answering questions such as "How does this work?" and "What causes this?" and "How can we improve this situation?" Here are the steps in the scientific method.

1. Decide which question to investigate.
2. Find the facts related to the question.
3. Form a hypothesis.
4. Perform an experiment to test the hypothesis.
5. Draw a conclusion.

Scientists are not the only ones who use the scientific method. You have probably used the scientific method in your everyday life. Imagine, for instance, that you have moved to a new neighborhood. You **ask the question** "What is the fastest way to get from my home to work?" You do not own a car, so you **find facts** about the bus and the subway—where each of them stops and how often each of them runs.

With these facts, you **form a hypothesis**, such as "Taking the subway is the fastest way for me to get to work." Now you **test your hypothesis by performing an experiment**. You take the bus to work for a few days. Then you take the subway to work for a few days. Next, you compare the average times for the two forms of transportation. With this information, you **decide whether your hypothesis was correct**. Now you know whether the bus or the subway will get you to work faster. By using the scientific method, you have solved an everyday problem in a careful, logical way.

Read the following passage to see how someone else used the scientific method to solve a problem.

Staying Warm: Wool or Cotton?

Masud worked in an ice-cream factory that was always cold. He wondered which would keep him warmer, a cotton sweater or a wool sweater. He knew that wool fibers have tiny pockets of air. He also knew that one of the best ways to keep warmth in an object is to surround that object with a thin layer of air.

Because of these facts, Masud thought a wool sweater would probably keep him warmer than a cotton one. He decided to test this guess with an experiment.

LANGUAGE *Tip*

Wearing a hat helps keep you warm. Your body protects your brain by keeping your head warm. When you cover your head, your body uses less energy to stay warm.

Masud filled two identical empty metal cans with boiling water. Then he wrapped a woolen sock snugly around one of the cans. He wrapped a cotton sock of the same thickness around the other can.

After 15 minutes, Masud unwrapped the cans. He felt each one. The can that had been wrapped in wool was warmer than the can that had been wrapped in cotton. Masud decided that his guess was right. Wool does a better job of keeping heat in a warm object.

Step 1 in the scientific method is defining the question you want to answer. Did you notice Masud's question? It was *Which will keep me warmer, a wool sweater or a cotton sweater?*

Step 2 is collecting facts that relate to the question. Which facts did Masud know? He knew that wool fibers contain pockets of air. He also knew that a layer of air helps hold in heat.

Step 3 is forming a hypothesis. What was Masud's hypothesis? It was that *a wool sweater would keep him warmer than a cotton one.*

Step 4 is performing an experiment. When Masud did his experiment, he did not use sweaters. But his experiment was a good test of this hypothesis. It compared cotton and wool socks of equal thickness.

Step 5 in the scientific method is to draw a conclusion about the hypothesis. What conclusion did Masud draw? He observed that the wool sock kept the can warmer than the cotton sock did. Therefore, he decided that his hypothesis was correct. A wool sweater would keep him warmer than a cotton sweater.

Strategy: The Five Steps of the Scientific Method

- Decide which question to investigate.
- Find the facts related to the question.
- Form a hypothesis, a logical explanation.
- Perform an experiment to test the hypothesis.
- Draw a conclusion about the hypothesis.

Exercise 1

Read the passage. Then circle the best answer for each question.

Sounds Strange to Me

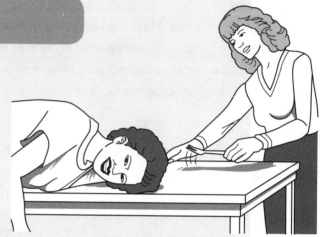

Tasha was floating on her back in the swimming pool. She noticed something strange. When her ears were underwater, sounds became very loud. When she splashed lightly with her hand, the noise she heard sounded like a huge paddle churning the water.

Tasha told her roommate what she had noticed. Her roommate was not surprised. She said sound vibrations travel more easily through water than through air. That is why sounds seem louder underwater. She said sound even travels more easily through wood than it does through air.

Tasha wondered about that fact. If her roommate was right, a noise would seem louder if you heard it through wood than if you heard it through air.

Tasha decided to test this hypothesis with an experiment. She had a wooden table in her kitchen. Tasha asked her roommate to tap the table lightly and steadily with a fork. Tasha listened for a few taps. The she pressed her ear against the table and listened some more. The sound seemed louder now. It was true—a sound does seem louder if you hear it through wood than if you hear it through air!

1. Which question did Tasha ask?
    (1) How can sound travel through wood?
    (2) Why does splashing water make a sound?
    (3) Does a fork make more sound in water or in wood?
    (4) Is sound louder if it travels through wood than through air?

2. Three of the statements below are facts that Tasha knew before doing her experiment. Which statement is *not* a fact?
    (1) Sound travels more easily through water than through air.
    (2) A sound that cannot be heard underwater can be heard through wood.
    (3) A sound seems louder if it travels through water than if it travels through air.
    (4) Sound travels more easily through wood than through air.

3. What was Tasha's hypothesis?
    (1) Sounds are clearest if heard underwater.
    (2) A noise will sound louder when heard through wood than when heard through air.
    (3) A noise will sound louder when heard through wood than when heard through water.
    (4) A noise will sound louder when heard through air than when heard through wood.

4. Which conclusion did Tasha draw at the end of her experiment?
    (1) Her hypothesis was correct.
    (2) Her hypothesis was incorrect.
    (3) Her roommate had been wrong.
    (4) Sound does not travel well through wood.

Check your answers on page 198.

Exercise 2

Do you have a hard time getting out of bed on a cold morning? This passage might help explain why.

Read the passage and answer the questions.

What Makes Some "Cold" Things Cold?

One cold morning, Don was trying to drag himself out of bed. He started wondering why it was so hard for him to get up on cold mornings. Why did the tile on the bathroom floor always feel so cold on his bare feet? Why did the bathroom rug not ever feel cold? He was sure that the tile and the rug must be the same temperature. After all, they were in the same room.

Then Don remembered what he had learned about heat. Heat can be conducted, or carried away. Some substances conduct heat better than others. Maybe the tile floor felt cold because tile was a better conductor of heat than the rug. Maybe the tile carried heat away from his feet more quickly than the rug did.

Don decided to test this guess with an experiment. He filled two empty soup cans with boiling water. Using potholders, he carried the cans into the bathroom. He placed one can on the rug and the other one on the tile floor.

Don waited a couple of minutes. Then he touched the can on the rug. It was still too hot for him to lift with his bare hand. Next he touched the can on the tile floor. It was cooler—cool enough to lift with his bare hand. The heat of the boiling water had been drawn away more quickly by the tile than by the rug. Don's hypothesis was right! The tile was a better conductor of heat than the rug was.

1. What question did Don want to answer?

_____

_____

2. Which facts did Don know that related to the question?

_____

_____

3. What hypothesis did Don form about the question?

_____

_____

4. Briefly describe Don's experiment in your own words.

_____

_____

_____

5. What conclusion did Don draw at the end of the experiment?

_____

_____

Check your answers on page 198.

Exercise 3

The sentences on the left tell a story. The phrases on the right describe the five steps of the scientific method. Match each part of the story with the correct step.

Exploring the Moon

_____ **1.** Scientists believed that people would jump higher and come down more slowly on the Moon than on Earth.

_____ **2.** Scientists concluded that their hypothesis was correct—where gravity is weaker, people can jump higher and stay up longer.

_____ **3.** For a long time, scientists wondered if people would look the same when they jumped on the Moon as when they jumped on Earth.

_____ **4.** In 1969, astronauts walked on the Moon for the first time. They found they could jump higher and stay up longer than on Earth.

_____ **5.** Scientists knew that gravity is the force that pulls things down toward the ground. They also knew that the Moon has much less gravity than Earth.

(a) deciding which question to investigate

(b) finding the facts related to the question

(c) forming a hypothesis

(d) performing an experiment to test the hypothesis

(e) drawing conclusions about the hypothesis

Check your answers on page 198.

Astronaut Edwin Aldrin Jr. walking on the Moon in 1969

Try It Yourself!

In this chapter, you have learned that sound travels more easily through some substances than through others. Do this experiment to learn more about sound.

What is the question?
How does sound change when you change the instrument making the sound?

Materials you will need
glasses or glass bottles
a spoon (for tapping the glasses)
liquids

Plan your investigation.
You have probably made a sound by blowing into a bottle. You can also make a sound if you tap on a glass containing a liquid. If you change the amount of liquid, the shape of the container, or the kind of liquid, you are changing your instrument.

Work with a partner. On the lines below, write your ideas for testing how sound changes when you change an instrument. Write something for each step of the scientific method. You will not be able to write a conclusion (step 5) until you have done your experiment.

You can continue this experiment by changing your instrument in various ways.

1. State the question: _____

2. State a fact related to the question: _____

3. Make a hypothesis: _____

4. Plan an experiment to test your hypothesis: _____

   _____

5. Draw conclusions: _____

Check your results on page 198.

Review – Physics

Most people do not think of daylight as having color. Would you believe that daylight really has several colors?

Read the passage. Then answer the questions that follow.

Is There Such a Thing as White Light?

Ping read an interesting statement: *White light is made up of red, green, and blue light.* This statement made her start wondering. Could you make white light by mixing red light, green light, and blue light? If what she read was true, Ping thought, you should be able to shine a red light, a green light, and a blue light on the same spot, and the three lights mixed together should make a white light.

Ping thought of a way to find out for sure. She took three flashlights. She taped red cellophane over the head of one of them. Then the flashlight gave off a red light when she shone it on a sheet of white paper. She taped green cellophane over the head of a second flashlight. Finally she taped blue cellophane over the head of the third flashlight.

Then Ping turned all three flashlights on at once. She pointed them so their lights fell on the same spot of the paper. She saw a white light, just as she had thought. Her hypothesis was correct. She found that you *can* make white light by mixing red, green, and blue lights.

Green

White

Red

Blue

1. Write *F* if the statement is a fact. Write *O* if it is an opinion.

    _____ **a.** It is interesting to know that white light contains red, green, and blue lights.

    _____ **b.** When Ping taped red cellophane over the flashlight, it produced red light.

    _____ **c.** Ping did an experiment to test her scientific ideas.

    _____ **d.** More people should experiment with science.

2. Which question did Ping want to answer?
    (1) How can you produce a green light with an ordinary flashlight?
    (2) Can you make a white light by mixing red, green, and blue lights?
    (3) What does white light contain?
    (4) How can you produce colored lights from white light?

3. Which fact about light did Ping know before she started her experiment?
    (1) The colors of light do not mix together in the same way that colors of paint do.
    (2) Sunsets are red because sunlight contains many different colors.
    (3) White light is made up of red, green, and blue lights.
    (4) People cannot see colors in dark rooms because there is not enough light.

4. What was Ping's hypothesis?
    (1) White light is made up of red, green, and blue lights.
    (2) It is possible to mix different colored lights together.
    (3) White light contains many different colors of light.
    (4) When red, green, and blue lights shine on the same spot, they produce a white light.

5. Which conclusion did Ping draw at the end of her experiment?
    (1) White light contains red, green, and blue lights.
    (2) You can make white light by mixing red, green, and blue lights.
    (3) It is possible to separate white light into different colors.
    (4) Colored light does not mix the same way colored paint does.

Check your answers on page 198.

Chemistry

Why do you need to shake a bottle of salad dressing before using it? Why does lemonade taste different when you add sugar? What happens when you heat a raw egg? These everyday questions are answered by a branch of science called **chemistry**.

Chemistry is the study of substances, or physical matter. Chemists study what substances are made of, what happens when they are combined, and how they can change. Believe it or not, you probably know more about chemistry than you think. Each time you cook a meal, for instance, you are mixing and changing substances.

Chapter	What You Will Learn About	What You Will Read
14	Cause and Effect	A Danger to Meats Milk: The Battle Against Germs The Chemistry of Key Lime Pie Solving a Problem with a Solvent
15	Predicting Outcomes	How Is Glass Made? From Paper to Pulp to Paper Help for the Gardener Making Your Own Ice Cream
16	Charts	Colloids Minerals Needed by the Human Body Fat in Milk and Milk Products What Happens at a Dump?
Review	Chemistry	Danger in the Air

After studying this unit, you should be able to

• recognize cause and effect

• predict outcomes

• read and understand charts

Chapter 14

Cause and Effect

Few things happen by accident. One event causes another event, that event causes a third event, and so on. A **cause** is whatever makes something happen. An **effect** is what happens as a result of that cause.

Why does milk turn sour? Why will oil and vinegar not stay mixed? What happens to plastic in a garbage dump? These are questions about cause and effect. Science can answer them.

Everyday life is full of causes and effects. Here is one example: *My car is being fixed, so I took the bus to work.* Do you see the cause and the effect in this sentence? The cause is *my car is being fixed.* The effect is *I took the bus to work.* The word *so* is a clue. It signals that an effect will follow.

Here is another cause-and-effect statement:

Wanda was late for work because she forgot to set the alarm.
      (EFFECT)   (CAUSE)

The word *because* is a clue. It signals that a cause will follow. Notice that the effect may be stated before or after the cause.

When you study science, you will read about causes and effects. You need to be able to recognize causes and effects. You should "see" in your mind which thing happened first and which thing happened as a result.

Practice finding causes and effects. In this paragraph, what happens first? What happens as a result?

A Danger to Meats

Today most cold cuts and hot dogs contain things besides meat. Almost all food companies add chemicals to their meats. Two of these chemicals are sodium nitrate and sodium nitrite. They keep meat from spoiling quickly. They also keep harmful **bacteria**, or germs, from growing in meat.

The paragraph states that food companies add sodium nitrate and sodium nitrite to cold cuts and hot dogs. That fact is a *cause*. The paragraph then states two *effects*. What are they?

_____

The effects of adding these chemicals are that *the meat does not spoil quickly and harmful bacteria do not grow in the meat.*

Now look for a cause and an effect in the next paragraph.

> Sodium nitrate and sodium nitrite add a new danger to meats. Scientists fed these chemicals to rats for long periods of time. The rats developed cancer. Scientists fear that sodium nitrate and sodium nitrite may cause cancer in human beings if people eat these chemicals over a long period of time.

This paragraph tells how scientists fed sodium nitrate and sodium nitrite to rats. That was the *cause* of an important *effect*. What is the effect?

_____

The effect is that *the rats developed cancer.*

Scientists fear sodium nitrate and sodium nitrite *may* have another effect. What is that effect?

_____

Scientists believe that *sodium nitrate and sodium nitrite may cause cancer in human beings.* The word *cause* signals the cause-and-effect relationship.

Strategy: How to Find Causes and Effects

- List all the events or facts.
- Look for words that signal cause and effect, such as *because, cause, since, due to, as a result, therefore,* and *so.*
- Think about which event happens first and which event follows.
- Remember that a cause can have more than one effect. Also, an effect can have more than one cause.

Exercise 1

Do you know why milk was once a deadly drink?

Read each paragraph. Write the causes and the effects in the space provided.

Milk: The Battle Against Germs

Until about 100 years ago, milk was often a dangerous drink. Everyone knew that milk quickly turned sour. But that was not the problem. The problem was that milk contained something strange. Because of that "something," people often became sick. Many people died after drinking milk.

1. **Cause:** Milk contained something strange.

   Effect: _____

During pasteurization, milk is heated to kill bacteria.

Milk is cooled so it stays fresh.

In 1864, a French scientist named Louis Pasteur made an important discovery. He learned that milk contained bacteria, or germs. These germs make the milk go sour. More importantly, Pasteur figured out that bacteria can cause deadly diseases.

2. Cause: _____

Effect 1: Milk went sour.

Effect 2: _____

Luckily, Pasteur also found a way to stop this danger. He heated milk quickly until it almost boiled. Then he cooled it quickly and kept it cool. As a result, the bacteria in the milk were killed.

3. Cause: Pasteur heated and cooled the milk quickly.

Effect: _____

Today almost all the milk that is sold is pasteurized. That means it is heated and cooled, just as Louis Pasteur did nearly 150 years ago. Because of this, milk stays fresh longer, and it is no longer a dangerous drink.

4. Cause: _____

Effect 1: Milk stays fresh longer.

Effect 2: _____

Check your answers on page 198.

Exercise 2

Key lime pie is a tasty dessert. Making a key lime pie is an example of using a chemical process.

Read each paragraph. Write the causes and the effects in the spaces provided.

The Chemistry of Key Lime Pie

One of the main ingredients of a custard pie is eggs. The eggs are beaten with sugar and flavorings, put into a pastry shell, and cooked. The heat changes the nature of the eggs in a significant way. What went into the oven as a liquid comes out as a solid. A chemical change occurs during the baking. The proteins in the egg are denatured by heat.

1. **Cause:** Eggs are heated.

   Effect: _____

There is more than one way to denature proteins. Adding an acid to the eggs has the same effect as adding heat. If you mix an acid with egg whites, the egg whites will quickly turn from a clear liquid to a solid white substance.

2. **Cause:** _____

   Effect: Egg whites change from a clear liquid to a white solid.

The fact that an acid can "cook" some foods without heat has resulted in a popular dessert—key lime pie. No one is sure who came up with the recipe. But most likely it was someone working on a fishing boat around the Florida Keys shortly before 1860. We know the place and the approximate year because of the main ingredients—key limes and sweetened condensed milk. Key limes grow only on the Florida Keys, the string of islands just south of Florida. Sweetened condensed milk was not available in cans until 1856.

3. Cause: _____

   Effect: Key lime pie was invented by someone in the Florida Keys.

4. Cause: Sweetened condensed milk was invented in 1856.

   Effect: _____

> Why do people believe that the inventor of key lime pie worked on a fishing boat? It is because of the cooking method used. At that time, boats fishing along the Keys were often out at sea for several days. Whoever prepared food for the crew could easily take along limes, canned sweetened condensed milk, and eggs. However, there was no oven onboard. There was no way to cook a pie with heat. But the citric acid in key limes is able to denature the eggs without heat. Traditional recipes for key lime pie do not require any cooking at all.

5. Cause: _____

   Effect: Traditional recipes for key lime pie do not require cooking.

> Today recipes for key lime pie call for cooking, but only for about 10 minutes. The cooking is done because of the health risk of eating uncooked eggs. The citric acid of the limes will denature the eggs, but it will not kill harmful bacteria that might be present. Cooking is recommended to kill the bacteria. It is not needed to harden the eggs.

6. Cause: The citric acid in key limes does not kill harmful bacteria in the eggs.

   Effect: _____

Check your answers on page 198.

Exercise 3

Here is a chemical tip to help you remove price stickers from the items that you buy.

Read each paragraph. Write the causes and the effects in the spaces provided.

Solving a Problem with a Solvent

Tiny bits of matter called **molecules** make up all the substances around you. Forces called **bonds** hold the molecules together. Bonds are like glue between molecules.

1. **Cause:** _____

   Effect: Bonds hold molecules together.

   Some bonds can be very strong. The glues on adhesive tape, price stickers, and stamps, for example, have very strong bonds. Because of their strong bonds, the glue molecules stick together tightly. Consider how hard it is to straighten a strip of tape that has folded on itself. The glue molecules can also stick tightly to other substances.

2. **Cause:** The glues on adhesive tape, price stickers, and stamps, have strong bonds.

   Effect 1: _____

   Effect 2: _____

   A **solvent** is something that can break, or dissolve, the bonds between molecules. Most solvents are liquid. To remove a price sticker from an item you bought, you need a solvent. It will break the bond between the glue molecules and the molecules of the item. Then the glue molecules will let go of the other molecules. They will link up with the solvent. Do not try to scrape away the sticker. Use a solvent!

3. **Cause:** _____

   Effect: A solvent can remove price stickers from items.

Check your answers on page 198.

Try It Yourself!

In this chapter, you have learned about substances that stick together and substances that break apart. Try this experiment to learn about which substances will combine with water to produce new substances.

Materials you will need

glasses

water

various substances (for example, cooking oil, dish soap, flour, fruit drink, cola, salt, sand, sugar)

spoon

Words you need to understand

In a *solution*, various substances are combined to produce a new substance. The original substances no longer exist.

In a *mixture*, various substances are combined, but the substances later separate into the original substances.

Steps

1. For each substance you will be working with, fill one glass with water.
2. Add one substance to each glass of water. Stir. (Be sure to wash your spoon before working with a new substance.)
3. Watch what happens right away. Record your findings.
4. Let the substance sit for five minutes. Record your findings.

You can continue this experiment by varying the amounts of a substance (such as sugar) that you add to the water. How do your results change when you change the amount of the substance that you use?

Write your conclusions

Identify the solutions and the mixtures you have produced.

Check your results on page 199.

Chapter 15

Predicting Outcomes

Scientists try to understand our world so they can guess what might happen in the future. It is not that scientists want to be fortune-tellers, but they want to know, for example, where a tornado might touch down. Or they want to know what will happen if someone takes a new medicine. In both cases, they want to **predict outcomes**—to guess what is likely to happen in the future.

You probably predict outcomes every day. Imagine that a severe storm is headed your way. Perhaps storms in the past have made your electrical power go out. It would make sense for you to guess that the power might go out this time too. On the basis of this prediction, you might stock up on candles and make sure your flashlight has batteries. You would be using your knowledge of the past to make a guess about the future.

Notice that a prediction is a reasonable guess. You can never be certain about what will happen in the future.

As you study science, you will learn many facts. You can use those facts to predict what might happen in the future. Try predicting as you read this passage and answer the questions.

How Is Glass Made?

Most glass is made from only three substances—sand, **soda,**[1] and **lime.**[2] These substances are mixed and heated in a furnace. There, they melt together into what looks like a clear syrup. When the syrup cools, it hardens into glass.

Sand is the most important ingredient in glass. Only small amounts of soda and lime are used. Soda is added because it makes sand melt at a lower temperature than it would without the soda. Lime keeps glass from dissolving in water.

---

[1]**soda:** a white powder sometimes made from salt

[2]**lime:** a white substance made from limestone

You can use these facts about glass to make some predictions. For instance, imagine that a glass company tried to make glass without soda. What would be the outcome?

To answer this question, think back to what you learned about why soda is added to glass. Soda makes sand melt at a lower temperature. Knowing this, can you predict the outcome if soda were left out? Circle the best prediction.

(1) The sand would not melt.
(2) The temperature would need to be higher before the sand would melt.
(3) The temperature would need to be lower before the sand would melt.

Statements (1) and (3) are not good predictions. The passage states that soda makes sand melt at a lower temperature than it would melt without soda. This tells you that the sand would melt even if no soda had been added. Without soda, however, the temperature would need to be higher before the sand would melt.

From these facts, you can guess that statement (2) is a good prediction.

Now imagine that the company left the lime out of a batch of glass bottles. What would happen once those bottles were filled with water? Circle the best prediction.

(1) The bottles would dissolve.
(2) The bottles would be strong.
(3) The bottles would change color.

Think back to what you learned about lime in the passage. Lime keeps glass from dissolving in water. From this fact, choice (1) is the best prediction. Glass made without lime would dissolve in water.

Strategy: How to Predict Outcomes

- List the facts that you know about the subject.
- Think about how things have happened in the past.
- Think about whether you expect the future to be different from the past or like the past.
- Make a reasonable guess as to what will happen. Base your guess on the facts you know or on what has happened in the past.

Exercise 1

Millions of people are now recycling paper instead of throwing paper away. How many times can paper be recycled?

Read the passage. Then answer the questions.

LANGUAGE Tip

Recycling 100 pounds of paper saves one tree. Saving one tree helps save the environment!

From Paper to Pulp to Paper

Americans produce about five pounds of waste per person each day. Paper makes up about one-third of all waste. Recycling paper is one important way to help the environment.

The first step in recycling paper is to soak it in water. This softens the paper **fibers** and separates them from one another. The result is a soupy mush called pulp. Next, the pulp is cleaned and dried. Finally, it is rolled into new paper.

Each time paper is broken down into pulp, its fibers become shorter and weaker. The paper made from these shorter fibers is not as strong as new paper. It tends to crumble and fall apart.

"Weak" paper is fine for some purposes. For example, it can be used for newspapers or toilet paper. But other products, such as envelopes and shopping bags, must be made from strong paper. For products like these, the pulp of recycled paper can be mixed with the pulp from new fibers that are longer and stronger. The paper made from this mix is stronger than paper made from only recycled fibers.

---

fibers: very thin threads

1. A paper company made shopping bags with paper that had been recycled several times. The company did not mix in any new fibers. Which of these statements is NOT a good prediction about the bags?
   (1) They will be brown.
   (2) They will be weaker than other shopping bags.
   (3) They will tear or break easily.
   (4) They will not last very long.

2. A fancy magazine was placed in a paper recycling bin. The magazine's paper is coated with a thin layer of plastic. The plastic keeps water from soaking into the paper. The plastic itself does not dissolve in water. What do you predict will happen when the magazine is soaked in water?
   (1) The paper will soak up water, and the plastic will pull away from the paper.
   (2) The paper's fibers will not soften or separate.
   (3) Plastic will become mixed into the paper pulp.
   (4) The recycled paper that is produced will be stronger.

3. Recycled paper usually costs less than new paper. A grocery store wants to print signs to hang in its windows. The signs need to last about one week. Which kind of paper do you predict the grocery store will use?
   (1) recycled paper
   (2) new paper
   (3) a mixture containing mostly new paper and some recycled paper
   (4) paper coated with plastic

4. A packaging company found that its envelopes made with recycled paper were too weak. The company decided to change the fiber content of these envelopes. What do you predict the company will do?
   (1) use more recycled fibers and fewer new fibers
   (2) use only recycled fibers
   (3) use more new fibers and fewer recycled fibers
   (4) keep the same number of recycled fibers and new fibers

Check your answers on page 199.

Exercise 2

How can knowing a little chemistry help you be a successful gardener?

Read the passage and complete the exercise.

LANGUAGE *Tip*

Homophones

Vary and *very* are homophones. They sound alike, but they are spelled differently.

vary	to change
very	truly

Help for the Gardener

Soils vary widely from place to place. Plants vary, too, in what they need from the soil. A good gardener tries to match plants with the conditions where they will be growing. Often that requires improving the soil in the garden. There are two important soil qualities that a gardener must consider—the soil's texture and its acid level.

Soil textures range from clay to sand. If you squeeze a handful of clay soil and then open your hand, the soil will stay in a hard, sticky mass. In the ground, clay soil holds water. It is hard for plants to send their roots into heavy clay soil. In addition, clay soil keeps roots wet for so long that they rot. However, if you squeeze a handful of sandy soil and then open your hand, the soil falls apart. Water falling on sandy soil drains through the soil quickly. Plants can send their roots into sandy soil easily, but when the soil dries out, the plants may die. Plants do best in soil that is neither all clay nor all sand.

The acid level in soil ranges from acid to alkaline. The acid level is measured by chemicals that are mixed with small samples of soil and water. If the soil is acid, the mixture turns one color. If it is alkaline, the mixture turns a different color. If the soil is neutral (neither acid nor alkaline), the color of the mixture appears to be between the other two colors. Some plants prefer acid soil, while other plants prefer alkaline soil. Most plants will do well in soil that is close to neutral.

The best way to improve soil texture is to add compost to the soil. Compost is a mixture of wastes such as vegetable peelings, leaves, and grass. In clay soil, compost breaks up the particles of clay so roots and water can get through the soil. In sandy soil, compost helps hold water so the soil will not dry out as fast. It also provides food for the plants. The best compost will not affect the acid level of the soil.

Another way to improve soil texture is to add peat moss to the soil. Peat moss is a special kind of moss that grows in wet areas. It holds water very well. To make an alkaline soil more acid, gardeners add peat moss to the soil. To lower the level of acid in soil, gardeners add lime.

1. Martin moves into a house with a yard full of plants. Acid-loving azaleas and alkaline-loving clematis grow next to each other. The azaleas look yellow and weak, while the clematis plants are bushy and full of flowers. Martin intends to test the acid level of the soil in the yard. What do you predict he will learn?

_____

2. The next fall Martin puts peat moss around the roots of the azaleas and clematis to protect the plants from snow. How will that affect the two plants? Will it help both plants or just one plant? Will it hurt both plants or just one plant? Predict the outcome of Martin's action.

_____

_____

3. Debra has planted tomatoes in her garden. Tomatoes do best in acid soils. Although Debra knew her soil was alkaline and sandy, she did not have time to improve the soil before putting in her plants. What do you predict about the size of her tomato crop?

_____

4. The following spring, Debra starts work in her garden early enough to improve the soil before planting. Which should she add: (1) only compost, (2) only peat moss, or (3) both? Predict which choice will give her the best crop, and explain why.

_____

_____

Check your answers on page 199.

Exercise 3

Some ice cream is rich and smooth. Other ice cream is full of ice crystals. What determines how smooth ice cream will be?

Read the passage and complete the exercise.

Making Your Own Ice Cream

Making a single serving of ice cream is surprisingly easy. The only ingredients are a tablespoon of sugar, a half teaspoon of vanilla, and a half cup of milk. In addition, you need two heavy-duty plastic bags that can be sealed, one small and one large. You will also need 6 tablespoons of salt and some ice.

Begin by putting the sugar, vanilla, and milk into the small plastic bag and sealing the bag. Then, place the small plastic bag into the large plastic bag. Next, fill the large bag half full of ice. Finally, add the salt to the ice, seal the large plastic bag, and shake it for 5 to 10 minutes. Then enjoy your frozen dessert.

This simple recipe includes the essentials of ice cream—milk fat, sweeteners, flavoring, and air. The milk provides the milk fat. The sugar serves as the sweetener. The vanilla adds flavor. Shaking the mixture in the plastic bags blends air into the mixture. The air is needed to make the ice cream foamy. Too much shaking, however, will turn the milk fat into butter. The ice and salt cool down the mixture enough to make it into a solid. But this approach works only on a very small amount—and the ice cream must be eaten soon after it is made.

To make larger amounts of ice cream that will keep well, three more ingredients are needed—nonfat milk solids (such as evaporated milk or milk powder), an emulsifier (such as eggs), and a **stabilizer** (such as gelatin). The nonfat milk solids give ice cream more body and help it hold air. The emulsifier helps the drops of milk fat mix more evenly with the water and air as the ice cream forms. The stabilizer keeps clumps of ice from forming when the ice cream is warmed and then refrozen.

1. At a restaurant that makes its own ice cream, the chef forgets to put eggs into one batch. What effect would you expect that mistake to have on the ice cream?
    (1)   The ice cream will not be sweet enough.
    (2)   The ice cream will not be smooth enough.
    (3)   Lumps of ice will form in the ice cream if it is taken in and out of the freezer.
    (4)   The quality of the ice cream will not be affected.

2. The same chef replaces the restaurant's usual strawberry flavoring with chocolate. What effect would you expect this change to have on the quality of the ice cream?
   (1) The ice cream will not be sweet enough.
   (2) The ice cream will not be smooth enough.
   (3) Lumps of ice will form in the ice cream if it is taken in and out of the freezer.
   (4) The quality of the ice cream will not be affected.

3. If the chef forgot to add gelatin to the ice cream, what effect would you expect it to have?
   (1) The ice cream will not be sweet enough.
   (2) The ice cream will not be smooth enough.
   (3) Lumps of ice will form in the ice cream if it is taken in and out of the freezer.
   (4) The quality of the ice cream will not be affected.

Check your answers on page 199.

 ## Try It Yourself!

In this chapter, you have learned how emulsifiers keep milk fat mixed evenly throughout ice cream. Try this experiment with an emulsifier you probably use every day.

Materials you will need
a clear bottle with a tight-fitting screw-on cap
water
cooking oil
food coloring
dishwashing liquid detergent

Steps
1. Fill the bottle half full of water. Add enough food coloring to make a bright color.
2. Pour in enough cooking oil so you can clearly see a layer of oil.
3. Cap the bottle, shake it, and set it down. Observe what happens to the oil and water.
4. When the oil and water have stopped moving, unscrew the cap. Pour a drop of detergent into the bottle. Cap the bottle again and shake. Observe what happens.

Draw your conclusions
What difference does detergent, an emulsifier, make? Why is it used to clean dishes?

Check your results on page 199.

Chapter 16

Charts

Information is often shown in **charts**. A chart lists facts in rows and columns. It may use words, numbers, or symbols. For example, look at the following chart. You have probably seen signs like this in store windows.

BUSINESS HOURS	
Monday	CLOSED
Tuesday	9–5:30
Wednesday	9–5:30
Thursday	9–9
Friday	9–7
Saturday	9–6
Sunday	11–4

This chart tells you when the store is open for business. You probably already know how to read it. First, find the day you want to know about. Then look at the numbers to the right. For instance, on Thursdays the store is open from 9:00 a.m. until 9:00 p.m.

Information about science is often given in charts. Look at the following example.

Colloids

Type of Colloid	Description	Example
fog	liquid mixed in gas	clouds
smoke	solid mixed in gas	smoke
foam	gas mixed in liquid	whipped cream
emulsion	liquid mixed in liquid	mayonnaise
sol	solid mixed in liquid	paint
gel	liquid mixed in solid	jelly

To read the chart, begin by looking at the title. It tells you that the chart gives information about **colloids**. A colloid is a mixture of two or more substances.

Next, read the **headings**. Headings are the titles for sections of the chart. The headings in this chart are *Type of Colloid*, *Description*, and *Example*.

Under each heading, you find more information. How many colloids are listed under the heading *Type of Colloid*?

There are six types of colloids listed: *fog*, *smoke*, *foam*, *emulsion*, *sol*, and *gel*.

Clouds are a mixture of a liquid and a gas.

Now look under the heading **Description**.
What is an emulsion? _____

An emulsion is *a liquid mixed in liquid*.

The final heading in the chart is *Example*.

What example is given of a gel? _____

The example of a gel is *jelly*.

As you can see, a chart can show a lot of information in a small space.

Strategy: **How to Read Charts**

- Read the title. It tells what the chart is about.
- Read all headings. They tell what information each section of the chart contains.
- Study the information under the headings.

Exercise 1

Study the chart and answer the questions.

LANGUAGE Tip

Computer Skill

To make a chart on the computer, go to the **Table** menu. Click **Insert** and **Table**. Then decide how many columns and how many rows you want in your chart.

Minerals Needed by the Human Body

Mineral	Main Purpose	Foods It Is Found In
calcium	strengthens bones and teeth	milk and milk products; dark-green leafy vegetables
magnesium	strengthens bones and teeth	dark-green leafy vegetables; nuts
phosphorus	builds and strengthens bones	milk, cheese, meat, fish
potassium	helps senses work well	fruits and vegetables; cereals
sodium chloride	keeps body chemistry balanced	salt
sulfur	needed to make hair and nails	meat, fish, eggs

mineral: a natural substance that is found in the ground

1. What is the main purpose of calcium in the body?

_____

2. Which other mineral has the same purpose as calcium?

_____

3. Which foods is calcium found in?

_____

4. Which mineral keeps body chemistry balanced?

_____

5. Which food is this chemical found in?

_____

6. Which two minerals are contained in milk and milk products?

_____

7. Which two minerals are contained in fish?

_____

8. What are the main purposes of those two minerals?

_____

_____

Check your answers on page 199.

Exercise 2

Milk products are healthy for us in many ways. They provide nutrients such as calcium, protein, and vitamins. But some milk products contain a lot of fat. Which milk products contain the most fat?

Study the chart. Then circle the best answer for each question.

Fat in Milk and Milk Products

Food	Serving Size	Fat (in grams)
Milk		
whole milk	8 ounces	8
2% milk	8 ounces	5
1% milk	8 ounces	2
skim milk	8 ounces	1
buttermilk	8 ounces	2
Butter and Cheese		
butter	1 tablespoon	11
cheddar cheese	1 ounce	9
creamed cottage cheese	4 ounces	9
low-fat cottage cheese	4 ounces	1
cream cheese	1 ounce	10
part-skim mozzarella cheese	1 ounce	5
Muenster cheese	1 ounce	9
Parmesan cheese	1 ounce	9
Swiss cheese	1 ounce	8
Frozen Dessert		
vanilla ice cream, rich	½ cup	12
vanilla ice milk	½ cup	3
sherbet	½ cup	4
Yogurt		
plain whole-milk yogurt	8 ounces	7
plain low-fat yogurt	8 ounces	4

gram: a measure of weight; a paper clip weighs about 1 gram

1. Which type of milk has the least fat?
   (1) whole milk
   (2) 2% milk
   (3) skim milk
   (4) buttermilk

8 Ounces
2% Milk

5 Grams
of Fat

2. Which of the following has the least fat?
   (1) a serving of cheddar cheese
   (2) a serving of part-skim mozzarella
   (3) a serving of Muenster cheese
   (4) a serving of Parmesan cheese

1 Ounce
Swiss Cheese

8 Grams
of Fat

3. According to the chart, how big is one serving of low-fat cottage cheese?
   (1) 4 ounces
   (2) 4 grams
   (3) 1 tablespoon
   (4) 1 teaspoon

1/2 Cup Rich
Vanilla Ice Cream

12 Grams
of Fat

4. How many grams of fat are in one serving of cream cheese?
   (1) 10 grams
   (2) 9 grams
   (3) 5 grams
   (4) 1 ounce

5. According to the chart, which dessert has the least fat?
   (1) rich vanilla ice cream
   (2) vanilla ice milk
   (3) plain whole-milk yogurt
   (4) plain low-fat yogurt

8 Ounces Plain
Low Fat Yogurt

4 Grams
of Fat

6. Which of the following has the most fat per serving?
   (1) whole milk
   (2) Swiss cheese
   (3) cream cheese
   (4) rich vanilla ice cream

Check your answers on page 199.

Exercise 3

Study the chart and answer the questions.

LANGUAGE *Tip*

Americans throw away 2.5 million plastic bottles every hour. Only about 20% of them are recycled. The rest will be in dumps for hundreds of years.

What Happens at a Dump?

Item	After One Year	After Five Years	Time Needed to Decompose[1]
paper milk carton	The carton flattens. Water makes it mushy.	The carton has decomposed.	5 years or less
aluminum can	Most of the paint has dissolved, but the can is still **intact**.[2]	The can is flat. It sinks into the soil.	80 years or more
plastic bottle	The bottle is almost the same as when it was thrown away.	Sunlight may have changed the bottle's shape, but it is intact.	500 years
Styrofoam food container	The container may have broken into several pieces.	All the pieces of the container are unchanged.	Styrofoam will never decompose.

[1]**decompose:** rot and slowly fall apart
[2]**intact:** in one piece; not broken apart

1. How will an aluminum can have changed after five years in a garbage dump?

   _____

2. How long does it take an aluminum can to decompose? _____

3. How will a plastic bottle have changed after five years in a garbage dump?

   _____

4. How much longer does it take a plastic bottle to decompose than a paper carton?

   _____

5. Several states require people to pay a tax every time they buy a product in an aluminum can. People can get their money back if they recycle the can. How does this tax help the environment?

_____

6. Some states are asking restaurants to stop using Styrofoam containers. Why do you think this is a good idea?

_____

7. Which of the objects listed in the chart decomposes the fastest? _____

8. Paper and aluminum are both made from natural substances. Plastic and Styrofoam are made with manmade substances. From what you read in the chart, which decomposes more quickly, natural or manmade substances?

_____

Check your answers on page 199.

Try It Yourself!

■ List two or three packaged foods that you buy often. They may be canned, such as soup. They may be wrapped, such as bread. Or they may be frozen, such as ice cream.

■ Go to the supermarket. For every food item on your list, find three brands or three types. For example, find three types of bread: white, whole wheat, and French.

■ Now look at the nutrition information printed on each package. Find the information on fat. How many grams of fat are in one serving of that food?

■ Make a chart to show what you found out. Then describe how the amounts of fat in the various foods are alike or different.

UNIT 4

Review – Chemistry

PART A

Once rainwater was pure and clean. Why has it changed?

Read the passage. Write the causes and the effects in the space provided.

Danger in the Air

Several countries, including the United States, have a serious problem in their forests. The leaves of many trees are drying up and falling off. Large numbers of trees have died. This problem is due to changes in the rain. The rain has become acid. Acid is a substance that can eat into certain things, such as leaves.

What made the rain acid? Factories, power plants, and cars all dump harmful substances into the air. Two of these substances are sulfur dioxide and nitrogen oxide. In the air, these two substances mix with tiny drops of water. They make the water acid. It falls to the ground as acid rain.

Because the rain is acid, leaves begin to die. Acid rain changes the soil that it falls on. As a result, the soil cannot feed the trees as it normally does.

1. **Cause:** Sulfur dioxide and nitrogen oxide mix with drops of water.

   Effect: _____

2. **Cause:** _____

   Effect: Leaves begin to die.

Circle the best answer.

3. Because of acid rain, several states have passed new laws. The laws put a limit on how much sulfur dioxide can be dumped into the air. What is a likely outcome of these laws?
   (1) In those states, there will be less acid rain than in the past.
   (2) In those states, there will be more acid rain than in the past.
   (3) In those states, people will decide not to drive cars as much.
   (4) In those states, new factories will be opened.

PART B

Study the chart. Then answer the questions.

SOME EFFECTS OF ACID RAIN AROUND THE WORLD	
Place	**Effect**
United States	75% of the lakes studied by the U.S. government contain acid.
Norway (Europe)	In the southern part of the country, most or all of the fish in many lakes have been killed. Plants and other animals have also died.
Greece (Europe)	In the last 20 years, acid rain has damaged ancient buildings and statues more than they have been damaged in the past 2,000 years.
China (Asia)	At least one-third of China is affected by acid rain. People in at least two-thirds of Chinese cities have serious health problems such as pneumonia.
India (Asia)	Heavy black clouds are seen over many cities. Farm products have decreased by 25%.

4. What is the effect of acid rain in Greece?

    _____

5. What has been the effect of acid rain on many lakes in southern Norway?

    _____

6. What is one important effect of acid rain in China?

    _____

Check your answers on page 200.

UNIT 5

Earth Science

What causes the weather? How do rivers change Earth's surface? Do people harm Earth when they cut down trees or kill insects? These are some of the questions answered by a branch of science called **Earth science.**

Earth science means many things. It is the study of weather and the seasons. It is the study of rocks, mountains, and rivers. And it is the study of how people change Earth—for good or for bad.

Chapter	What You Will Learn About	What You Will Read
17	Identifying Problems and Solutions	Saving Water for a Dry Day Blowing in the Wind Ozone Alert! Tsunami Warning System
18	Using Prior Knowledge	Earth's Wear and Tear *and* A Clean Slate The Earth Beneath Our Feet Acid Rain Lost in the Clouds
19	Line Graphs	Ohio Temperatures World Population Growth Daylight Hours Solid Waste
20	Bar Graphs	Tornadoes Elevation Forest Fires Precipitation
Review	Earth Science	The Problem with DDT *and* Water Use

After studying this unit, you should be able to

• identify problems and solutions

• use what you already know to understand new situations

• read and understand graphs

Chapter 17

Identifying Problems and Solutions

Scientists often search for ways to solve problems. "Why is my child not growing as fast as others her age?" "How can I water my crops when it has not rained for months? "Why are so many trees in the forests dying?" These are examples of real-life problems that scientists try to solve.

We all know what it is like to face problems. In general, we do our best to find solutions. Perhaps you moved a lot of heavy objects. You ended up with a problem: a sore back. What could you do? You might try several solutions: taking two aspirins, using a heating pad, or resting. If those solutions did not work, you had to see a doctor.

As you study science, you learn about many problems and the solutions people use to solve the problems. You will not learn about all the ways scientists *tried* to solve the problems that failed. Often you read only about the solutions that finally worked. The fact is, many scientists can spend many years searching for the solution to one problem.

Read this passage. Can you find the problem and the solution?

Saving Water for a Dry Day

In some parts of the world, several months often go by with no rain. Rivers that may be full at some times of the year become dry. The result can be a dangerous shortage of water. This water shortage can kill crops, animals, and even people.

To avoid such dangers, people build dams. A dam ensures that there will be enough water, even in a dry spell. This is how a dam works.

Normally the water in a river flows without stopping. Eventually all the water flows into a larger river or an ocean. A dam is built to hold back some of the river's water. It lets only some of the water flow through. A large, deep pool of river water forms behind the dam. This pool is called a reservoir.

When a dry spell comes, people can use the water in the reservoir. If water is needed downstream from the dam, some of the water in the reservoir can be let out. That water will flow downstream, following the river's normal path. In this way, a dam can help people "find" water when there is a water shortage.

What problem does the passage describe? Write your answer on this line.

_____

You could have answered *a dangerous water shortage* or *a long time without rain.*

What solution is described in the passage? _____

The correct answer is *a dam.*

How does a dam solve the problem of a dangerous water shortage? The dam forms a reservoir. If people near the dam need water, they can take water from the reservoir. If people downstream need water, some water can be let out of the reservoir. The water will flow where it is needed.

Dams control the amount of river water that flows downstream.

Strategy: How to Identify Problems and Solutions

- To find the problem, ask yourself, "What was wrong?"
- To find the solution, ask yourself, "What was done to change things?"
- Be sure you can explain how the solution solved the problem.

Exercise 1

For years, scientists have been warning us about dirty air. Why is our air so dirty? What can we do to clean it? Here is one answer.

Read the passage. Then circle the best answer for each question.

Blowing in the Wind

Cars, televisions, toasters, phones, lamps—we use dozens of machines in our daily lives. What makes these machines run?

Most machines run on fossil fuels—oil, coal, and natural gas. Gasoline is made from fossil fuel. Cars, airplanes, and other engines run by burning gasoline. Most of our electricity is made by burning fossil fuel.

When fossil fuels burn, they give off gases. Some of these gases cause acid rain. Other gases are slowly heating up our air. This is as dangerous as acid rain.

Is there any way out of the fossil-fuel mess?

Here is one way out: the wind. Wind does not cost anything. It does not **pollute**. Wind can be used to turn windmills. Those windmills can produce electricity. In hundreds of places around the world, people have built windmills to make power without polluting.

Wind probably cannot solve all of our energy problems. Wind does not blow all the time. Some people feel windmills clutter up the land, but chances are windmills will become more common. They are a lot cleaner than the burning of fossil fuels.

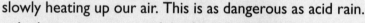

pollute: harm the air, water, or land

LANGUAGE Tip

Many Texas ranches are becoming wind farms. One very large windmill can supply electricity to 500 homes.

1. Which are examples of fossil fuels?
   (1) electricity and coal
   (2) oil, coal, and natural gas
   (3) gasoline and electricity
   (4) electricity and windmills

2. According to the passage, what is the main problem with fossil fuels?
   (1) They are hard to find in the earth.
   (2) They are expensive.
   (3) They give off gases when they are burned.
   (4) They cannot make as much electricity as we need.

3. What has been one harmful effect of the gases produced by burning fossil fuels?
   (1) acid rain
   (2) the cooling of the air
   (3) the burning of gasoline
   (4) the production of electricity

4. Which solution to this problem is described in the passage?
   (1) using fewer machines
   (2) reducing the amount of dangerous gas produced by fossil fuels
   (3) using windmills to produce electricity
   (4) making more machines that do not run on electricity

5. How does this solution solve the main problem of fossil fuels?
   (1) It does not cause pollution.
   (2) It is cheaper than fossil fuels.
   (3) It can produce more electricity than fossil fuels do.
   (4) It is easier to find than fossil fuels.

Check your answers on page 200.

Chapter 17

Exercise 2

How can there be a hole in the air? Why is that hole dangerous?

Read the passage and complete the exercise.

Ozone Alert!

There is a blanket of air surrounding Earth. This blanket, which is called the "atmosphere," is about 300 miles thick. Above the atmosphere, there is no air—there is just empty space.

About 25 miles above Earth is a layer of ozone gas. The ozone layer screens out most of the ultraviolet light from the sun. This ultraviolet light causes painful sunburn. Too much ultraviolet light can be deadly.

In the 1980s, scientists noticed something happening to the ozone layer. It was becoming thinner. Then scientists discovered a large hole in the ozone layer above the South Pole and a smaller hole above the North Pole. Something was destroying the ozone.

This "something" was a group of chemicals called chlorofluorocarbons, or CFCs. When CFCs are released into the air, they slowly rise higher and higher. When they reach the ozone layer, they destroy the ozone.

Before 1980, CFCs were used in refrigerators, freezers, and air conditioners. Fire extinguishers and Styrofoam cups and boxes also contained CFCs. There were CFCs in spray cans containing paint, deodorant, and cleaning products.

During the 1980s, more and more people around the world became worried about the dangers of CFCs. In 1987, leaders from many countries came together to sign a treaty agreeing to ban CFCs by 1996. More countries signed the treaty later. After twenty years, 191 countries had signed the treaty.

Is the treaty helping to get rid of the hole in the ozone layer? Scientists say it is. In 2007, the hole in the ozone layer was the smallest it had been in five years. However, the ozone layer has not yet recovered.

Some countries still have not signed the treaty. They continue using CFCs. In addition, a few countries that signed the treaty are not keeping their promise. They are still using CFCs. Even when everyone stops using CFCs, the effects of CFCs will last a long time. It takes many years for CFCs to break down and disappear. Scientists say that it will take fifty years or more before the ozone layer is repaired. Nevertheless, scientists say we have made a good start at solving the problem. Our actions are saving the layer that protects life on Earth.

1. Which problem is caused by chlorofluorocarbons (CFCs)?
   (1) Ozone, which keeps sunlight away from Earth, is produced.
   (2) Some countries use CFCs in refrigerators and freezers.
   (3) CFCs can burn skin and kill living things.
   (4) CFCs destroy the ozone layer.

2. The destruction of the ozone layer causes
   (1) the sky to be cloudy
   (2) days to be longer
   (3) harmful sunlight to reach Earth
   (4) the temperature to drop

3. Which two things happened in the 1980s to help solve the ozone problem?
   (1) More people became concerned about the problem.
   (2) Leaders of countries signed a treaty banning CFCs.
   (3) Companies made Styrofoam cups with CFCs.
   (4) The hole in the ozone layer is the smallest it has been in five years.

4. According to the passage, there are three reasons why it will take a long time to solve the ozone problem. Which of these is NOT a reason?
   (1) Some countries are still using CFCs.
   (2) A few countries that promised not to use CFCs are still using them.
   (3) People care more about CFCs than the ozone layer.
   (4) CFCs take years to break down and disappear.

Check your answers on page 200.

Exercise 3

When ocean waves rise suddenly, people near the shore are in great danger. What can be done to protect people?

Read the passage and complete the exercise.

LANGUAGE Tip

tsunami   soo-NAH-mee

The word *tsunami* comes from the Japanese language. It means "harbor wave."

Tsunami Warning System

On December 26, 2004, a tsunami hit the coast of the Indian Ocean. A tsunami is a series of huge waves. It is often started by an underwater earthquake. These waves can travel thousands of miles across the sea. When they hit land, they are strong enough to destroy buildings, trees, animals, and people. The 2004 tsunami destroyed thousands of homes and boats. It killed more than 225,000 people.

Many of those people might have been saved if there had been a warning system. In order to warn people about a tsunami, however, there must be a way to discover when a tsunami is coming. There must also be a way to send out news so people will have time to move to a safe place. Neither of these problems is easy to solve.

It is difficult to predict when a tsunami will happen. Scientists know when an earthquake occurs. However, a tsunami warning cannot be sent out every time there is an earthquake because not every earthquake causes a tsunami. Many warnings would be false alarms. Then people might stop paying attention to the warnings.

Even if scientists believe there will be a tsunami, they still have the problem of how to warn people. There are many ideas of how to spread the news of a possible tsunami. The warnings could be sent out by loudspeakers or sirens. Alarms could be announced on the radio and television. Police officers could go house-to-house warning people. Warnings could even come by phone or e-mail. However, it is hard to know exactly which areas will be in danger. Some of the people who would be hit by a tsunami are very poor. They may not have televisions or e-mail. Some who could be hurt live in small villages. These villages are unlikely to have warning systems.

Scientists and government officers are working on an international tsunami warning system. They want to avoid the kind of disaster that happened in 2004. They hope to have a system in place before another tsunami strikes. They know their work is important. A good warning system can save thousands of lives.

1. According to the passage, which of the following could save lives when there is a tsunami?
   (1) teaching people how to swim
   (2) a tsunami warning system
   (3) a wall to prevent the tsunami from hitting land
   (4) a way to stop underwater earthquakes

2. Which of the following is NOT mentioned as a way to warn people about a tsunami?
   (1) putting up signs
   (2) having an announcement on the radio
   (3) going from one house to another and telling people
   (4) using a siren

3. Why is it difficult to have a tsunami warning system? _____

4. What problem do scientists have in predicting a tsunami? _____

Check your answers on page 200.

Try It Yourself!

In this chapter, you have learned about air pollution. This experiment will help you see the pollution in the air around you.

Materials you will need
heavy paper or cardboard
sticky tape or stick-on labels
string

Steps
1. From the heavy paper or cardboard, make several cards about 3"-by-5" long.
2. In the center of each card, cut a window about 2½"-by-1¼" big.
3. Attach a string to the top of each card so the card can be hung up.
4. Cover the window of each card with sticky tape or a stick-on label. Work from the back of the card so the sticky surface faces the front of the card.
5. Hang the cards in various places.
6. After a few days, take down the cards. Look carefully at what you have collected. Write a brief description of what you have found in the air you breathe.

Chapter 18

Using Prior Knowledge

Most of us like to feel that the things we learn are useful. After working hard to learn math, you feel good when your math skills help you figure out the final price of a sale item. This is just one example of using prior knowledge. **Using prior knowledge** means using what you already know to solve a problem or to understand a new situation.

What you learn in science will help you understand the world around you. Using prior knowledge can help you think about new situations.

You know that Earth's surface is constantly changing. But do you know why?

Read the following passage.

Earth's Wear and Tear

Erosion is the wearing away of Earth's surface. Erosion is caused by weathering—wind, rain, and temperature changes that break up rocks and move soil. Two types of weathering occur in nature: mechanical weathering and chemical weathering.

Mechanical weathering breaks rocks into smaller pieces. For instance, the Sun's heat may cause a rock to expand and split. Water may freeze on a rock's surface. The expanding ice may crack the rock.

Mechanical weathering can also be caused by wind. When the wind blows hard, it picks up pieces of rock and soil and carries them along. This driving wind can cut away at rocks. The rocks become worn away. Then they split apart more easily.

Chemical weathering is a change in the minerals inside a rock. This usually happens when water is present. Water can wash away the minerals in a rock. This weakens the rock. Also, rain mixed with carbon dioxide can dissolve rocks such as limestone.

Keep in mind what you learned about weathering in this passage. Now read the next passage. How does what you learned about erosion relate to what you are reading?

A Clean Slate

Sandblasting is a way to clean the outside of brick or stone buildings. A high-powered stream of sand is blown against the brick or stone. As the sand hits the surface, it removes the dirt that has settled on the stone.

Although sandblasting is a sure way to clean brick, it has its drawbacks. It often weakens the brick. Over time, the bricks can crumble. The process also leaves bricks and stones more porous. This means that they are more likely to absorb water, and water causes damage. For these reasons, sandblasting is often used as a last resort.

Use what you learned about erosion to think about sandblasting. Circle the best answer.

Sandblasting is like erosion caused by
  (1)   water
  (2)   temperature change
  (3)   wind
  (4)   the sun

You read that sandblasting is sand being blown against the surface of a brick wall. This is most similar to erosion caused by (3), *wind*.

Now think about what you know about sandblasting. Answer this question.

What material cleans the stone surface?
  (1)   water
  (2)   sand particles
  (3)   ice
  (4)   air

Did you choose (2)? The passage says that sand removes dirt from the stone. The high-powered stream of sand causes this erosion. Sandblasting, then, is an example of mechanical weathering. In the same way that wind cuts away at rocks and hills, sandblasting cuts away at the outer layer of bricks.

Strategy: How to Use Prior Knowledge

- Ask, "What do I know that relates to the new situation?"
- Identify things in the new situation that are similar to or different from what you already know.
- Draw a conclusion.

Chapter 18 Using Prior Knowledge   **153**

Exercise 1

Have you ever used the phrase "on solid ground"? There is no such thing. Whether you feel it or not, the ground is always moving.

Read the passage. Then circle the best answer for each question.

LANGUAGE Tip

Each year there are more than 2 million earthquakes. However, most earthquakes cannot be felt. Usually only one of these earthquakes is a major quake (rated 8 or higher on the Richter scale).

The Earth Beneath Our Feet

Most of us think of land as quiet and unchanging. In fact, most of Earth is made up of bubbling, boiling liquid. The land that we live on is only the outside crust of the planet. It is a thin layer floating on Earth's boiling, churning center.

The outside crust is not solid. It is made up of pieces called tectonic plates. Tectonic plates also form the bottom of lakes, rivers, and oceans. Some of the plates are huge. They cover spaces as big as the Pacific Ocean. Other plates are much smaller.

Since the plates are floating, they can bump into each other. When they do, they may slide past each other without causing any harm. But it is not always that smooth.

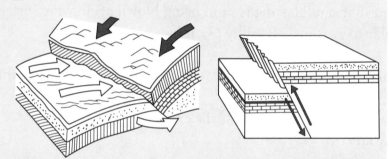

When two tectonic plates grind together, earthquakes can occur.

Moving plates may rumble and shake. Their edges may grind together and break. Does that sound like an earthquake? That is what it is.

Most earthquakes happen at the point where tectonic plates meet. The edge of one plate may rise while the edge of the next plate falls. Events like this can carve a cliff in what was once flat ground.

During an earthquake, the land may also crack open. A volcano may appear. A volcano is a vent, or opening, in Earth's crust. Boiling-hot liquid and gas can spurt from this vent. Most volcanoes form at the edges of tectonic plates. They tend to form in the same areas where earthquakes occur.

1. What are tectonic plates?
   (1) the boiling, churning center of Earth
   (2) cliffs or vents in Earth's crust
   (3) lakes, rivers, and oceans on Earth
   (4) pieces that form the outside crust of Earth

2. The city of Bella Vista, California, lies where two tectonic plates meet. A new 20-story building is being planned for Bella Vista. Using the information in the passage, what do you think this building should be like?
   (1) It should be as narrow as possible.
   (2) It should be able to sway a little without caving in.
   (3) It should be built across the two plates.
   (4) No buildings should be erected on this site.

3. If you want to build a skyscraper in an earthquake-active area, you should take into account
   (1) how often the earthquakes occur
   (2) how strong the earthquakes are
   (3) neither (1) nor (2)
   (4) both (1) and (2)

4. Millions of years ago, Mount George erupted. This mountain is located on Vancouver Island, in western Canada. It lies where two tectonic plates meet. Mount George has not erupted since that time. Using the information in the passage, what can you predict?
   (1) The plates under Mount George have probably stopped moving.
   (2) Mount George will never erupt again.
   (3) Mount George will probably have an earthquake, but it will not erupt.
   (4) Mount George may have an earthquake, or it may erupt again.

Check your answers on page 200.

Exercise 2

When plants do not get enough rain, they die. However, some plants die because of the rain that falls on them. How can this be?

Read the passage and complete the exercise.

LANGUAGE Tip

These words come from the Latin words that mean "through mud."

pollute   make dirty
pollution dirt in air, soil, or water
polluter   someone who makes air, soil, or water dirty
pollutant something that makes air, soil, or water dirty

Acid Rain

All living things need water. Rain provides the water needed by plants and animals. In many places in the world, however, rain has become dangerous. This dangerous rain is the result of pollution in the air and acid gases from factories and cars. It is called *acid rain.*

Acid gases are made when fossil fuels (such as coal, oil, and gasoline) are burned in power stations, factories, cars, and homes. When fuels are burned, gases are released into the air. Once the gases are in the air, they rise and mix with tiny droplets of water in clouds. The rain that falls from these clouds is full of acid. This is why it is called "acid rain."

Acid rain can be carried over long distances. The acids go high in the air. Then they are pushed from one area to another—even from one country to another. Acid can be found in snow, sleet, fog, and hail as well as rain.

Acid rain harms everything it falls on. When it falls on a forest, it can cause trees to grow more slowly or to die. When it falls on a lake, fish and other animals are affected. Their bones, shells, and eggs become deformed. Many animals die. Soon nothing is alive in the lake.

Acid rain can also ruin buildings and statues. The acid eats into metal and stone. Many famous buildings have been damaged by acid rain. The Acropolis in Greece and the Taj Mahal in India are examples of buildings that are being destroyed by acid rain. More damage has been done to these buildings in the last 20 years than in the previous 2,000 years.

Scientists are trying to solve the problem of acid rain. They are designing cars that do not burn fossil fuels. They are searching for sources of energy that will produce less pollution. They are asking everyone to use less electricity. When less electricity is used, there is less pollution from power plants. When there is less pollution in the air, there is less acid rain.

1. What is acid rain?
   (1) rain containing a high level of acid
   (2) rain that harms forests, lakes, and buildings
   (3) harmful rain caused by pollution
   (4) all of the above

2. Which of these two activities would be most likely to contribute to the creation of acid rain?
   (1) taking a walk
   (2) driving your car
   (3) keeping your TV on all day
   (4) eating a sandwich

3. Which two activities can you do to help reduce the acid rain problem?
   (1) carpool to work
   (2) do not go swimming in a lake affected by acid rain
   (3) live out in the country
   (4) turn off lights when you are not using them

4. You are the owner of a factory. What can you do to help solve the acid rain problem?
   (1) There is nothing you can do because the problem is too big.
   (2) Use wind power instead of power made from fossil fuels.
   (3) Run your factory at night instead of during the day.
   (4) Move your factory to an area where it does not rain often.

Check your answers on page 200.

Exercise 3

What really happens when it rains? When it snows? When it hails?

Read the passage. Then circle the best answer for each question.

Lost in the Clouds

Do you know how rain is formed? It begins when the sun warms the water in lakes, rivers, and oceans. Some of that water evaporates and becomes gas called **water vapor**. It rises into the air. When enough water vapor is in the air, clouds form.

In the clouds, the water vapor cools down. Then the water vapor changes back into **droplets**, or tiny drops, of water. The droplets begin to stick together. They become bigger and heavier. Finally, the droplets fall to Earth as rain.

Often the high part of a cloud is so cold that the water vapor changes into ice crystals. If it is cold, those crystals may fall as snow. If the weather is mild, the crystals pass through warm air as they fall to the ground. They melt and change into rain.

Sometimes ice crystals meet warmer air on their way to the ground. They partly melt. Then a draft of air blows them back up into the cold air. The ice crystals freeze again. The crystals may continue moving up and down. As they do, droplets of water stick to them. That water also freezes, and the crystals grow bigger. The stronger the draft of air, the longer the crystals continue moving up and down in the air.

When the crystals are heavy enough, they fall to Earth. This is what we call hail. For hail to form, there must be a layer of warm air under a layer of cold air. There must also be drafts of wind blowing upward.

1. Which event occurs first during the formation of rain?
   (1) Clouds form.
   (2) Water in lakes, rivers, and oceans evaporates.
   (3) Water vapor cools down in the clouds.
   (4) Water droplets stick together.

2. In general, spring is the season when there is the most chance of having a layer of warm air under a layer of cold air. Therefore, spring usually has
   (1) about the same number of hailstorms as other seasons
   (2) fewer hailstorms than other seasons
   (3) more hailstorms than other seasons
   (4) no hailstorms

3. There was a hailstorm today. The upward drafts of air were much stronger than normal. The hailstones were probably
   (1) harder than normal
   (2) wetter than normal
   (3) bigger than normal
   (4) smaller than normal

4. You know that rain is formed from evaporated water. In which of these places is it most likely to rain often?
   (1) near an ocean in a warm climate
   (2) in the desert
   (3) near a river in a cold climate
   (4) in the mountains

Check your answers on page 200.

Try It Yourself!

In this chapter, you read about how rain, snow, and hail form. Try this experiment to learn how rain and fog are formed.

Materials you will need
glass jar
small plastic sandwich bag
very hot water
ice cubes

Steps
1. Fill the jar with very hot water. After 1 minute, pour out most of the water. Leave about 1 inch of hot water in the jar.
2. Put 10 ice cubes in a small plastic bag, and seal it. Place the bag on the top of the jar.
3. Watch what happens. Describe the results.

Check your results on page 200.

Chapter 19

Line Graphs

Graphs are used in science to show information. Like diagrams and charts, graphs can give a lot of **data**[1] in a small amount of space. Graphs can also show comparisons between things.

There are several kinds of graphs. One of the most common graphs is the **line graph**. As you might guess, it uses lines to show information. Study this example.

Ohio Temperatures

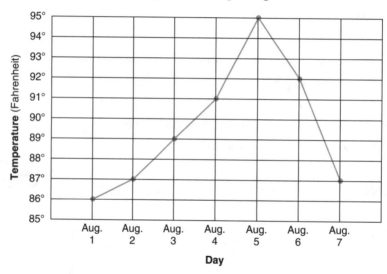

High Temperatures in Oakdale, Ohio
August 1 through August 7

Begin by reading the title. It tells you what the graph is about—the high temperatures in Oakdale, Ohio, from August 1 through August 7.

Next, read the labels on the graph. Start on the left with the **vertical**[2] label. It says **Temperature (Fahrenheit)**. Near the label are numbers that stand for temperatures. Find 85°. It is located next to the bottom line. This means that the bottom line stands for 85 degrees Fahrenheit. Next to the top line, you see 95°. This means that the top line stands for 95 degrees Fahrenheit. Each line between the top and the bottom stands for a different temperature.

---

[1]**data:** facts
[2]**vertical:** straight up and down

LANGUAGE Tip

This chart will help you compare degrees centigrade with degrees Fahrenheit.

0°C = 32°F
10°C = 50°F
20°C = 68°F
30°C = 86°F
40°C = 104°F
100°C = 212°F

Below the **horizontal**[3] line at the bottom of the graph, you see dates. The graph uses the abbreviation *Aug.* for August. Find the date August 3. Follow the line up from that date. Where the August 3 line crosses the 89° line, there is a dot. The dot means that the high temperature on August 3 was 89°.

Now find August 4 on the graph. Follow the August 4 line up to the dot. The dot is on the 91° line. The dot means that the high temperature on August 4 was 91°.

Notice that a line joins the August 3 dot and the August 4 dot. This line goes up. It shows that the temperature was higher on August 4 than on August 3.

Find the line joining the August 5 dot and the August 6 dot. The line goes down. That shows that the temperature was lower on August 6 than on August 5.

Now you see how to read a line graph–you follow lines to figure out information.

Try it yourself. Use the graph to answer these questions.

What was the high temperature on August 2? _____

When you follow the August 2 line up, you see a dot on the line for *87°*.

How did the temperature change between August 6 and August 7?

_____

Between August 6 and August 7, *the temperature went down.* You can tell this because the line between these two points slopes downward. It was warmer on August 6 than on August 7.

---

[3]**horizontal:** right to left

Strategy: **How to Read Line Graphs**

- Read the title. It tells what the graph is about.

- Look at the labels. They tell what information is on the graph.

- Study the line. See where it goes up and where it goes down. The line helps you see how things changed.

Exercise 1

Study the graph. Then circle the best answer for each question.

World Population Growth

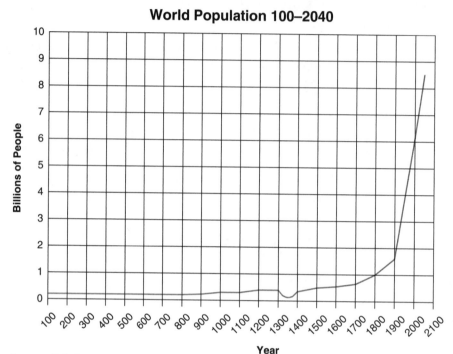

World Population 100–2040

Source: U.S. Census Bureau

1. What do the numbers next to the left (vertical) line stand for?
   (1) years
   (2) hundreds of people
   (3) millions of people
   (4) billions of people

2. What do the numbers along the bottom (horizontal) line stand for?
   (1) years
   (2) hundreds of people
   (3) millions of people
   (4) billions of people

3. Which statement best compares world population in the year 100 with the population in the year 1100?
   (1) It was about the same.
   (2) It was much larger in the year 1100.
   (3) It was larger in the year 100.
   (4) It was above 1 billion in both 100 and 1100.

4. In the year 1700, the world population was
   (1) just over 1 billion
   (2) under 1 million
   (3) under 1 billion
   (4) over 2 billion

5. The population reached 1 billion in about the year
   (1) 1700
   (2) 1800
   (3) 1900
   (4) 2000

6. World population decreased about the year
   (1) 1150
   (2) 1350
   (3) 1550
   (4) 1750

7. In the year 2000, world population was about
   (1) 6 million
   (2) 7 million
   (3) 5 billion
   (4) 6 billion

8. What general trend in population growth can you tell from the graph?
   (1) The world's population has not changed much since A.D. 100.
   (2) The world's population has grown rapidly each century since A.D. 100.
   (3) The world's population has decreased since A.D. 100.
   (4) The world's population remained small from 100 to 1700 and then grew rapidly.

Check your answers on pages 200–201.

Exercise 2

What is the topic of this graph? What do the labels on the graph tell you?

Study the graph and complete the exercise.

Daylight Hours

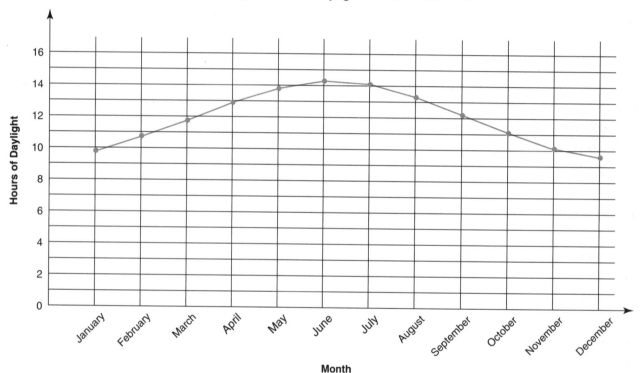

Average Hours of Daylight for San Francisco

1. Which two months have more than 14 hours of daylight per day?

   _____   _____

2. Which two months have between 10 and 11 hours of daylight?

   _____   _____

3. Which month has the most hours of daylight? _____

4. Which month has the fewest hours of daylight? _____

5. About how many hours of daylight are there in October? _____

6. How many hours of daylight will there be on January 15 (to the closest full hour)?

   _____

7. Approximately how many more hours of sunlight does May have than January?

   _____

8. Which month has more hours of daylight, April or September? _____

9. The sun rose at 7:15 a.m. on December 12. Will it set before or after 5:15 p.m.?

   _____

10. How many months have more than 12 hours of daylight per day? _____

Check your answers on page 201.

Exercise 3

Study the graph and answer the questions.

Solid Waste

Solid Waste Produced in U.S.Cities, 1960–2000*

Millions of Tons (y-axis)

Year (x-axis)

*not including construction waste, industrial process waste, and some other wastes

Source: Environmental Protection Agency, 2003

1. In which year were about 90 million tons of solid waste produced?

    _____

2. In which year were about 120 million tons of solid waste produced?

    _____

3. About how many tons of solid waste were produced in 2000?

_____

4. How has the amount of solid waste produced in U.S. cities changed since 1960?

_____

Check your answers on page 201.

Try It Yourself!

Make a line graph of your own. Check TV news, a newspaper, or an online weather site to find the daily high temperature where you live (or where you would like to visit). Keep a record for seven days in a row.

Then make a line graph to show your record. Begin by writing in the dates across the bottom. Each vertical line should stand for one day.

Next, put a dot on the line for the high temperature that day. Use the horizontal lines to find the place for each dot.

Finally, draw lines to join the dots. Your graph is finished!

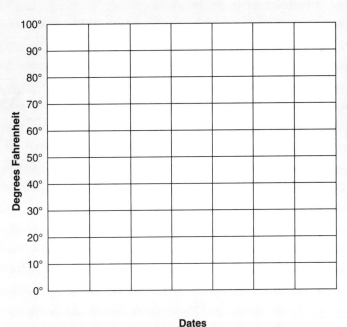

Draw your conclusions

Study your graph. In one or two paragraphs, summarize the data that it shows. What trends can you see? Has the temperature gone up, gone down, or stayed the same?

Chapter 20

Bar Graphs

Another common type of graph is the **bar graph**. It uses bars of different lengths to show information. Study this example.

Tornadoes

What is the graph about? The title tells you that the graph's topic is the average number of tornadoes each month in the United States from 2004 through 2006.

Look at the horizontal line across the bottom of the graph. You see the months of the year. Above each month is a bar. The bar shows the average number of tornadoes in the United States during that month.

Next, look at the numbers on the vertical line on the left side of the graph. The label says that each line represents the number of tornadoes. Find the line labeled 80. If a bar reaches that line, it means that an average of 80 tornadoes occurred during that month.

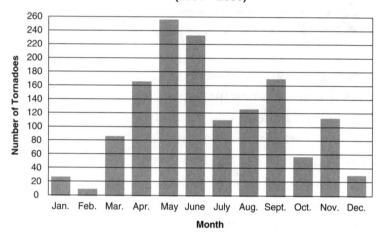

Average Number of Tornadoes Each Month in the United States, (2004 – 2006)

Source: National Weather Service, 2007

Find the bar for the month of June. It reaches a little more than halfway between 220 and 240. On the average, more than 230 tornadoes occurred during the month of June.

Now find the bar for August. It reaches almost halfway between 120 and 140. On the average, there were almost 130 tornadoes in the United States during August.

Can you read the graph yourself? Answer these questions.

Between 2004 and 2006, what is the average number of tornadoes that occurred in the United States in February? _____

The bar for February reaches halfway between 0 and 20. The correct answer is *10*.

What was the average number of tornadoes in May?

_____

LANGUAGE Tip

A tornado is a dark cloud that can spin as fast as 300 miles per hour. A tornado sounds like a train. To protect yourself, go to a basement or to a room with no windows.

The bar reaches almost to the 260 line. You should have answered *about 260*.

Bar graphs let you compare things at a glance. To compare the average number of tornadoes in April with the average number of tornadoes in May, you do not need to look at the numbers on the left side of the graph. You can just compare the size of the bars. The bar for May is taller than the bar for April. Therefore, May had more tornadoes, on the average, than April.

To answer the following questions, compare the length of the bars.

In which month were there more tornadoes— July or August? _____

Your answer should have been *August*. The August bar is taller than the July bar.

In which month did the fewest tornadoes occur? _____

The correct answer is *February*. That month has the shortest bar.

Strategy: *How to Read Bar Graphs*

- Read the title. It tells what the graph is about.
- Real the labels. They tell what information is on the graph.
- Study the bars. They show the facts, and they help you compare things quickly.

Exercise 1

Study the graph and answer the questions.

Elevation

LANGUAGE Tip

On May 29, 1953, Edmund Hillary and his guide were the first people to reach the top of Mt. Everest, the world's tallest mountain. Today about 500 people reach the top of Mt. Everest every year.

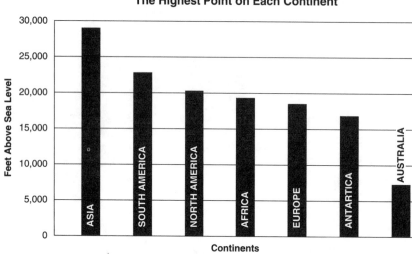

The Highest Point on Each Continent

1. What do the numbers on the vertical line on the left of the graph stand for?
   (1) the size of each continent
   (2) the number of mountains on each continent
   (3) the number of feet above sea level
   (4) the number of feet on each continent

2. What do the bars along the horizontal line at the bottom of the graph stand for?
   (1) the number of feet above sea level
   (2) the continents
   (3) the population
   (4) the number of mountains on each continent

3. Which continent has the highest point? _____

4. Which continent's highest point is the lowest? _____

5. The highest point in North America is about 2,000 feet lower than the highest point in

   which continent? _____

What is the highest point on each continent? Write the correct letter on the line provided.

_____ 6. Africa

_____ 7. South America

_____ 8. Asia

_____ 9. Australia

_____ 10. North America

_____ 11. Europe

_____ 12. Antarctica

(a) 29,028

(b) 7,310

(c) 20,320

(d) 22,834

(e) 16,864

(f) 18,510

(g) 19,340

Asia's Mount Everest is the highest peak in the world.

13. What hypothesis about Australia can you make if you know that Australia's highest point is only 7,310 feet high?

_____

Check your answers on page 201.

Wild fires are a problem in California because much of the land in that state is desert. What can you learn about California fires from this graph?

Study the graph and complete the exercise.

Forest Fires

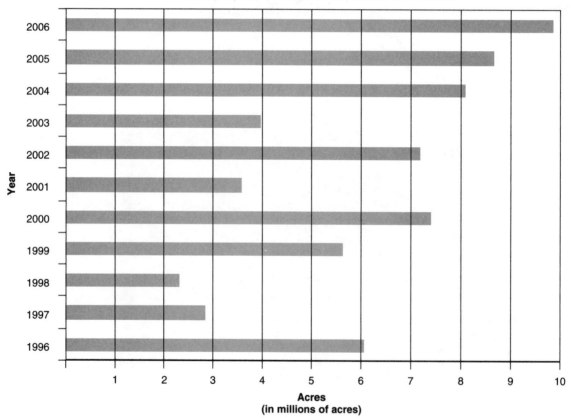

Forest Land Burned in California Fires

How many acres were burned in each of the following years? Write the correct letter on the line provided.

_____ 1. 1996   (a) 2,329,704

_____ 2. 1998   (b) 8,097,880

_____ 3. 2000   (c) 9,873,745

_____ 4. 2001   (d) 7,393,493

_____ 5. 2004   (e) 6,065,998

_____ 6. 2006   (f) 3,570,911

7. In which year were the fewest acres burned? _____

8. In which year were the most acres burned? _____

9. In which two years were 3 million to 4 million acres burned?

_____

10. In how many years were 5 million acres or more burned? _____

11. Which statement can you make after studying the information on the graph?
    (1) A year with many fires is always followed by a year of few fires.
    (2) In four of the last five years shown on the graph, there were major fires.
    (3) There are more fires every year.
    (4) There are not enough firefighters in California.

Check your answers on page 201.

Exercise 3

Study the graph and answer the questions.

Precipitation

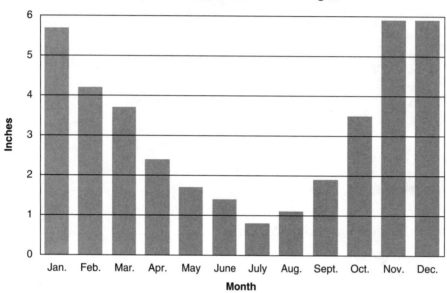

Average Precipitation (Rain or Snow) per Month in Seattle, Washington

What is the average precipitation in each month? Write the correct letter on the line provided.

_____ **1.** March   (**a**) about 3½ inches

_____ **2.** May   (**b**) almost 6 inches

_____ **3.** July   (**c**) more than 1½ inches

_____ **4.** October   (**d**) less than 1 inch

_____ **5.** November   (**e**) more than 3½ inches

6. The most precipitation occurs during which two months?

_____

7. The least precipitation occurs during which month? _____

8. On the average, how much precipitation is there in April?

   _____

9. Is there more precipitation in April or September?

   _____

10. Which season would be considered the dry season in Seattle?

    _____

Check your answers on page 201.

Writing Workshop

Prewriting
Think about the following questions. Then choose one question to write about.
1. Does your home town have a dry season?
2. Does your home town get a lot of rain or snow?
3. Do you think your home town has a pleasant climate?

Drafting
Write a topic sentence that states the main idea of your paragraph. Then expand on that idea by giving details that describe the climate in your town.

Revising
All the sentences in your paragraph should relate to the topic sentence. Delete sentences that will not help the reader understand your main idea. Be sure your last sentence restates the main idea in a new way.

Editing
Look for compound sentences (two complete sentences joined by *and*, *but*, or *or*). Be sure you have used a comma after the first part of the sentence.

   Example: The winters are cold, but the summers are not too hot.

Review—Earth Science

PART A

Few people like bugs. Would it matter if all bugs are killed?

Read the passage and answer the questions.

The Problem with DDT

There are millions of insects in this world. Some, like bees and ladybugs, help people. Others, like grasshoppers, are harmful. Some harmful insects eat the crops that farmers plant. Some spread diseases. People try to get rid of insects in many ways. One way is to use insecticides. Insecticides are poisons that kill insects.

DDT is one kind of insecticide. Farmers started using DDT in the 1940s. It did a good job of killing bugs quickly. The farmers were happy that insects were doing less damage to their crops. Then they began to use more DDT.

It turned out that DDT was not just killing bugs. It was also killing birds, fish, and other animals. This is what happened. Farmers would spray their fields with DDT. Small animals would eat grass and leaves that had been poisoned with DDT. These small animals would be eaten by larger animals. The poison built up in the animals' bodies. Many animals died. Others were unable to reproduce. DDT killed many thousands of birds, especially bald eagles. Some kinds of birds were almost wiped out.

People finally saw how bad DDT was. They did not want farmers to use it any more. In 1972, the United States passed a law forbidding the use of DDT. Thanks to this law, some kinds of birds that were in danger of dying out are now recovering.

DDT was not used just in the United States. It was used all over the world. People everywhere became upset about DDT. In 2001, many countries signed a treaty about the use of insecticides. However, this treaty does not ban DDT entirely. Some countries in Asia and Africa still use DDT to kill mosquitoes. Mosquitoes spread malaria, a disease that kills more than 1 million people every year. Health officials in these countries know that DDT is dangerous, but they believe they need to use DDT to save lives.

Scientists are looking for a new insecticide. It must be as good as DDT at killing bugs, but it must be safer than DDT. Everyone is hoping that DDT will soon be replaced. Until then, DDT will continue to be a problem as well as a solution.

1. Why do farmers use insecticides? _____

2. What problem can DDT cause? _____

3. What did the United States do to solve this problem? _____

4. Why do some countries still use DDT? _____

5. Some foods imported from Africa to a local African restaurant are found to have harmful chemicals. From what you have learned in the passage, what is one possible reason for this?

_____

PART B
Study the graph and answer the questions.

Water Use

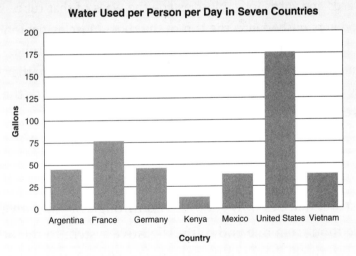

Water Used per Person per Day in Seven Countries

Source: Association of American Geographers, 2007

1. Which country uses the most water per person? _____

2. About how much water do the people in that country use? _____

3. Which country uses the least water per person? _____

4. About how much water do the people in that country use? _____

Check your answers on page 201.

Posttest

This Posttest will help you check how well you have learned the skills that will help you read science materials. You should take the Posttest after you have completed all the exercises in this book.

You can check your answers on page 191. Then fill out the Posttest Evaluation Chart on page 190. The chart will tell you which sections of the book you might want to review.

Could you eat lunch while standing on your head?

Read the passage and answer the questions.

How Food Gets to Your Stomach

Gravity pulls things down toward the ground. What would happen if you ate while you were upside down? Would the food reach your stomach? Or would you have to stand right side up before eating?

Look at the diagram on the next page. It shows the digestive system. The parts of this system work to break down food so the body can use it. The digestive system is mostly a tube, yards and yards long. Muscles line the walls of that tube.

When you swallow, food gets pushed into the top of the tube. Muscles tighten up to squeeze against the ball of food. They push the food farther into the tube. Then the next muscles squeeze the same way. They push the food a little farther. And so it goes, all the way through the digestive system. These muscles work the same way whether you are right side up or upside down.

You can eat whether you are hanging upside down or sitting at a table. You can eat a meal—or even sip a drink through a straw!

1. Which statement best summarizes how food travels through the digestive system?
   (1) Gravity pulls the food from one end of the digestive system to the other.
   (2) The food falls from the highest point of the digestive system to the lowest point.
   (3) Muscles push food through the digestive tube.
   (4) The food on top pushes down the food below it.

2. There is no gravity in outer space. How do astronauts eat in space? Use the facts in the passage to choose the most reasonable answer.
   (1) They cannot digest food normally.
   (2) They must sit up while eating.
   (3) They must eat with their feet pointing toward Earth.
   (4) They digest their food normally.

3. When the muscles of the digestive system squeeze against food, what effect does that have on the food?

_____

Study the diagram and answer the questions.

THE DIGESTIVE SYSTEM

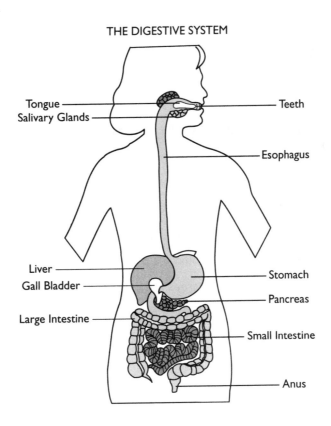

Tongue
Salivary Glands

Teeth

Esophagus

Liver
Gall Bladder

Stomach

Pancreas

Large Intestine

Small Intestine

Anus

4. When food is swallowed, where does it go after it passes the mouth?

_____

5. What is the last part of the digestive system that food goes through before it reaches the anus?

_____

How do weather forecasters decide which term to use to describe wind? Below is the scale that most forecasters use.

Study the chart and answer the questions.

Beaufort Wind Scale

Speed (miles per hour)	Description	Effects
less than 1	calm	smoke rises
1–4	light air	smoke drifts
5–7	light breeze	leaves rustle; weather vanes move
8–11	gentle breeze	leaves and twigs move
12–18	moderate breeze	small branches move; light flags fly extended
19–24	fresh breeze	small tree branches move; loose paper lifts
25–31	strong breeze	small trees sway
32–38	near gale	large tree branches move
39–46	gale	whole trees move; walking is hard
47–54	strong gale	shingles blow off roofs
55–63	storm	trees are uprooted; buildings may be damaged
64–73	violent storm	widespread damage
74 and over	hurricane	very widespread damage

6. How fast do winds blow in a hurricane? _____

7. Which is more dangerous—a storm or a gale? _____

8. You live in a small house with a satellite dish on the roof. Next to the house stands a tree. The wind is blowing 50 miles per hour. What effects do you predict?

_____

_____

Have you ever seen a bug walk on water? What is the trick?

Read the passage and answer the questions.

The "Thin Skin" of Water

One day when Dave was fishing on a lake, he noticed something strange. Small leaves that fell onto the lake floated on top of the water. They did not sink. He also saw tiny bugs that seemed to dance on the surface of the water. Dave wondered how that could be. Why didn't the leaves and the bug sink into the water?

Then Dave learned that the surface of water has a "skin," which is called surface tension. Dave thought that this skin might be keeping the leaves and the bugs from sinking.

Dave did an experiment to find out whether his idea was right. He took a small paper clip and a cup filled with water. He bent up one end of the paper clip to form a small handle. Then he gently laid the paper clip onto the water. It floated! Dave proved that surface tension could keep a paper clip from sinking. Surface tension must be able to hold up leaves and bugs.

9. Which question did Dave ask?
    (1) How can you keep things from sinking in water?
    (2) How many paper clips can float on water?
    (3) How can leaves and bugs float on water?
    (4) What breaks the "skin" of water?

10. What was Dave's hypothesis?
    (1) Bugs and leaves are lighter than paper clips.
    (2) Surface tension can keep leaves and bugs from sinking.
    (3) A paper clip is lighter than a leaf or a bug.
    (4) Water's "skin" is not very strong.

11. What conclusion did Dave draw at the end of his experiment?
    (1) His hypothesis was correct.
    (2) His hypothesis was true for paper clips but not for bugs or leaves.
    (3) Surface tension is stronger in a cup than in a lake.
    (4) A paper clip is as light as a bug.

What did the world look like millions of years ago?

Read the passage and answer the questions.

One World, One Continent

Scientists believe that at one time, Earth's seven **continents**[1] were joined in one great land mass. They call that continent Pangaea (pan-JEE-uh). Pangaea broke apart long ago. Slowly the pieces of this large continent drifted to where they are now.

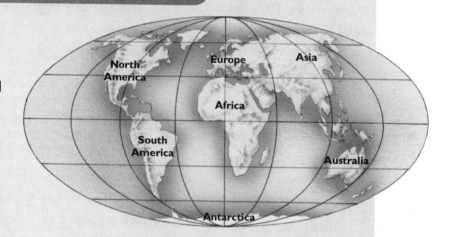

Do you find this idea hard to believe? Look at this map of today's continents. Can you see how South America and Africa almost fit together like pieces of a puzzle? That is one piece of evidence for the Pangaea hypothesis.

There is more evidence supporting the idea. Many kinds of rock lie in layers under the ground. **Geologists**[2] have found layers of rock in South America that match rock in Africa. It is as if someone made a sandwich with lots of layers and then cut the sandwich in half. How could the layers of rock be so much alike unless they were once joined?

Fossils[3] also suggest that the continents were once joined. An animal called a mesosaur lived about 200 million years ago. The mesosaur is now extinct. Fossils of this animal have been found in both South America and Africa. There is no sign that mesosaurs ever lived anywhere else in the world. A huge ocean now lies between South America and Africa. Could the mesosaur have crossed an ocean? It does not seem likely that the mesosaur swam across the ocean but went nowhere else in the world. This is another reason why scientists think the two continents were probably joined at one time.

[1]**continents:** large masses of land
[2]**geologists:** scientists who study Earth
[3]**fossils:** the remains of plants or animals that lived long ago

12. Pangaea is

    (1) a scientist who studies Earth

    (2) an animal that lived about 200 million years ago

    (3) a rock found in both South America and Africa

    (4) a continent that may have once existed

13. The passage presents the hypothesis that

    (1) all of Earth's continents were once joined

    (2) rocks found in Africa were brought from South America

    (3) mesosaurs swam across the ocean between South America and Africa

    (4) mesosaurs once lived on all seven continents

14. What evidence supports the hypothesis in question 13?

    (1) The mesosaur died out about 200 million years ago.

    (2) Rock layers in South America and Africa are similar.

    (3) People can still see the continents moving.

    (4) The continents were once joined together.

15. What are two important ways in which Africa and South America are alike?

    a. _____

    b. _____

16. According to the theory about Pangaea, how do Earth's continents differ now from the continents millions of years ago?

    Now: _____

    Millions of years ago: _____

    _____

Has a plant done anything for you lately? Chances are that it has.

Read the passage and answer the questions.

Plants and Medicines

Through the ages, people have used plants to ease pain and cure sickness. They have ground seeds to make healing powders. They have boiled leaves to make soothing tea.

Many people still use plants in this way. Some of these people live in far-off places. They may never have heard of modern medicines such as aspirins.

But many modern medicines come from plants too. Digitalis (di-ji-TAL-iss) is one example. It is made from the leaves of a flowering plant called the foxglove. For hundreds of years, digitalis has been used for people with weak hearts. Today we still use it for that purpose.

In time past, Native Americans made tea from the bark of a willow tree. The tea could kill pain. Modern scientists studied the willow bark. They found it contained a substance called salicin (SAL-uh-sin). Salicin is now used to make aspirin.

There are still thousands of plants that no one has ever studied. Many of these plants have never even been named. Scientists are searching for these plants. They are studying them in hopes of finding new medicines. Who knows what cures may be found right under our feet?

Foxglove growing in Idaho

17. Which sentence best expresses the main idea of the passage?
    (1) In times past, people had to use plants for medicine.
    (2) Our medicines are very different from medicines of the past.
    (3) In times past, people had almost as many medicines as we have today.
    (4) In times past and today, many medicines have been made from plants.

18. Scientists have just begun to study an Indian tribe that lives in a South American jungle. The tribe uses a certain plant to ease toothaches. Scientists had never heard of the plant before. Given the facts in the passage, what should the scientists do?
    (1) Tell the Indians that aspirin would be a better medicine for toothaches.
    (2) Study the plant to see if it could be useful for other people too.
    (3) Tell the Indians that they should take better care of their teeth.
    (4) Try to get everyone to use that plant instead of aspirin.

Write _F_ if the statement is a fact and _O_ if it is an opinion.

_____ 19. People were better off hundreds of years ago when all their medicines came from plants.

_____ 20. Digitalis was used as a heart medicine hundreds of years ago, and it is still used for that purpose today.

_____ 21. Scientists are trying to find more plants that can be used for medicine.

You may have seen the word *biodegradable* on a shopping bag or a food package. What is biodegradable? What is not?

Read the passage and answer the questions.

What Happens to Garbage?

What happens to garbage after we throw it away? It usually decomposes, or rots. Our garbage—our banana peels and used paper and whatever else we throw out—is being broken down into tiny pieces. It will take time, but those tiny pieces will become part of the soil. That is a good thing. We would not want the world to be overcome with piles of trash. Unfortunately, not all our garbage will decompose quickly. Some of our garbage may be around for thousands of years.

You may have noticed when you are near a garbage dump that garbage does not smell good. The smell is due to **microbes**. Microbes are living things that we can see only by looking at them under a microscope. These hungry microbes eat the garbage. As they do so, they change the garbage into a new substance. The microbes eat the items in our trash that were once alive, like apple cores or orange peels. They also feed on those items that were made from living things. For example, they eat paper, which is made from trees. During the process, they give off gases that do not have a pleasant odor.

Products that are eaten by microbes are **biodegradable** (BYE-oh-dee-GRAYD-uh-bul). Biodegradable products can be broken down easily. However, many items that we throw away are not biodegradable. The cans and plastic bottles for our soft drinks are not biodegradable. Glass bottles and Styrofoam cups are other examples of products that do not break down quickly. It will take hundreds or even thousands of years for those products to decompose.

What happens to garbage after we throw it away? Usually we just forget about it, but some of that garbage is not going away. It will be with us for a long time.

22. What is the main idea of this passage?

    (1) Microbes cause many things in a garbage dump to decompose.
    (2) Most things in a garbage dump are biodegradable.
    (3) Most things in a garbage dump are not biodegradable.
    (4) Everything in a garbage dump will decay if you wait long enough.

23. Which word or phrase is the best definition of the word *decomposition*?

    (1) the process of rotting
    (2) microbes
    (3) something that can be eaten by microbes
    (4) garbage that used to be living things

24. A town has a garbage dump that is almost full. The people in the town would like to make the garbage in the dump decay faster. According to the facts in the passage, what might be a good solution to their problem?

    (1) Do not let people dump garbage made from animals or plants.
    (2) Try to kill as many of the microbes as possible.
    (3) Try to keep the garbage separate from the microbes.
    (4) Ask people to use more biodegradable products.

25. Number the events in the order in which they happen.

    _____ Garbage starts breaking down into a new substance.
    _____ A smelly gas is given off.
    _____ Microbes begin feeding on garbage.

26. Use the information in the passage to complete the chart.

Category	Biodegradable	Not Biodegradable
Features	1. 2.	1. 2.
Examples	1. 2. 3.	1. 2. 3.

Study the graph and answer the questions.

Cancer

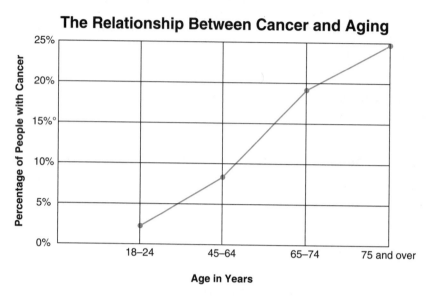

The Relationship Between Cancer and Aging

Source: Centres for Disease Control, 2005

27. By what age would about 20% of the population expect to have had cancer?
    (1) 8–24 years old
    (2) 45–64 years old
    (3) 65–74 years old
    (4) 75 years and older

28. According to the graph, which statement is most likely true?
    (1) People under 18 years of age do not get cancer.
    (2) People under 18 years of age have a low rate of cancer.
    (3) Very old people all have cancer.
    (4) Most people die of cancer.

Study the graph and answer the questions.

Snack Foods

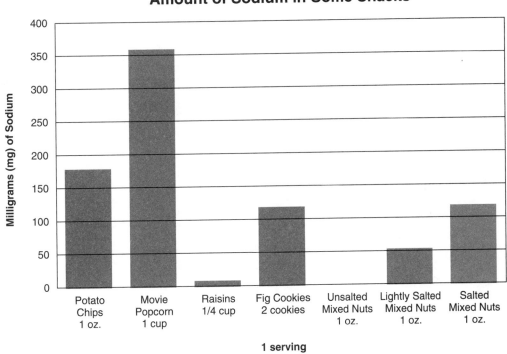

Amount of Sodium in Some Snacks

29. Which contains more sodium—a serving of movie popcorn or a serving of salted mixed nuts?

_____

30. If you are trying to reduce the sodium in your diet, what type of snacks would be best?

_____

Check your answers on page 191.

Posttest Evaluation Chart

Use the Posttest Answer Key on page 191 to check your answers. Next, find the number of each question you missed. Circle that number in the Item Number column of this chart. Then write the number of correct answers you had for each skill. If you need more practice in any skill, refer to the chapter that covers that skill.

Chapter	Skill	Item Number	Number Correct
1	Details	12	
2	Main Idea	17, 22	
3	Summarizing	1	
4	Sequence	25	
5, 10	Diagrams	4, 5	
6	Restating Facts	23	
7	Comparison and Contrast	15, 16	
8	Classifying	26	
9	Drawing Conclusions	2	
11	Facts and Opinions	19, 20, 21	
12	Making a Hypothesis	10, 13, 14	
13	The Scientific Method	9, 11	
14	Cause and Effect	3	
15	Predicting Outcomes	8	
16	Charts	6, 7	
17	Problems and Solutions	24	
18	Using Prior Knowledge	18	
19	Line Graphs	27, 28	
20	Bar Graphs	29, 30	

Posttest Answer Key

1. (3) This process is described in the passage.

2. (4) The muscles of the digestive system push the food through the digestive tube. It does not matter what position the body is in.

3. It pushes the food farther into the digestive tube.

4. through the esophagus

5. the large intestine

6. 74 miles per hour or faster

7. A storm; its winds are 55 to 63 miles per hour. A gale's winds are only 39 to 46 miles per hour.

8. The tree might move and twigs might break off. The satellite dish might blow off.

9. (3)   11. (1)   13. (1)

10. (2)   12. (4)   14. (2)

15. a. They have matching layers of rock.

    b. They both have mesosaur fossils.

16. **Now:** There are seven separate continents.

    Millions of years ago: All the continents were joined in one land mass.

17. (4)   19. O   21. F   23. (1)

18. (2)   20. F   22. (1)   24. (4)

25. 2; 3; 1

26.

Category	Biodegradable	Not Biodegradable
Features	1. made of something that was once alive 2. Microbes will eat it.	1. made of things that were never alive, such as metal, glass, clay, or plastic 2. Microbes will not eat it.
Examples	1. banana peels 2. apple cores 3. paper	1. plastic or glass bottles 2. cans 3. Styrofoam cups

27. (3) Nearly 20% of all people who are 65–74 years old have had cancer.

28. (2) Although the graph does not give information about people who are under 18 years old, the curve of the line helps you draw the conclusion that very few in this age group have had cancer.

29. **Popcorn;** movie popcorn has more sodium than nuts, even salted nuts.

30. **Raisins and unsalted nuts;** these foods are natural products that contain little or no sodium.

Answer Key

Unit 1: Human Biology

Chapter 1: Finding Details

Exercise 1, pages 6-7
1. (4) 3. (4) 5. (3)
2. (2) 4. (2)

Exercise 2, pages 8-9
1. (4) 3. (1) 5. (3)
2. (2) 4. (4)

Exercise 3, pages 10-11
1. tiny organs in the skin that can sense touch, pressure, pain, and temperature
2. the brain
3. The eye is very delicate, so it has more pain receptors than other parts of the body.
4. They warn us about danger so we can protect ourselves.

Try It Yourself! page 11
You most likely squeezed the ball fewer times when your muscles were cold than when they were warm. If you did several trials, you probably also noticed that you squeezed the ball fewer times when your muscles were tired.

Chapter 2: Finding the Main Idea

Exercise 1, pages 14-15
1. (3) 3. (4) 5. (2)
2. (3) 4. (1)

Exercise 2, pages 16-17
1. (3) 3. (1)
2. (2) 4. (4)

Exercise 3, pages 18-19
1. (3) The other choices are all true statements, but they are details. Choice (3) is the main idea that pulls together all these details.
2. (2) Choice (1) is true, but it is a detail. Choices (3) and (4) are incorrect.
3. (4) Choices (1), (2), and (3) are true, but they are details. Choice (4) sums up all the details.

Try It Yourself! page 19
You should have found it quicker and easier to work with two eyes open. Each eye sees something a little different. When your two eyes are working together, you are able to see in three dimensions (height, width, and depth).

Chapter 3: Summarizing

Exercise 1, pages 22-23
1. (3) Only choice (3) retells all the important points in the paragraph.
2. (1) Choice (1) is the only sentence that retells all the important points presented in the paragraph.
3. (3) All the other choices are true statements, but only choice (3) summarizes all the important points.

Exercise 2, pages 24-25
1. (1) Choices (2), (3), and (4) restate only one fact.
2. (2) Choice (2) briefly retells all the important points.
3. (4) Only choice (4) summarizes all the important points.
4. (3) Choices (1), (2) and (4) restate only one detail.

Exercise 3, page 26
1. (4) Choices (1) and (2) are too general. Choice (3) restates only one fact. Choice (4) retells all the important points.
2. (2) Choices (1) and (3) leave out several important points. Choice (4) is a restatement of only one fact. Choice (2) briefly retells all the important points.

Try It Yourself! page 27
Many people will be able to identify all the foods by sight. They may be able to identify many foods by tastes. Most people will have difficulty identifying many foods by smell.

Chapter 4: Putting Events in Sequence

Exercise 1, pages 30-31
1. 2, 4, 1, 3, 5
2. (a) the skin is hot
   (b) sending messages to the sweat glands
   (c) dries on the skin
3. 5, 2, 4, 1, 3
4. When you break a bone, first, soon, next, in time, once the callus is complete, finally

Exercise 2, pages 32-33
1. 2, 4, 5, 1, 3
2. (1)   4. (2)   6. (3)
3. (2)   5. (4)

Exercise 3, pages 34-35
Blood travels from the heart to the lungs, where the blood (1) picks up oxygen and (2) turns bright red. Then, it travels to (3) the heart and to (4) all other parts of the body, where the blood does these two things: (5) gives out all its oxygen and (6) turns dark reddish blue. Finally, it travels to (7) the heart, where blood (8) begins a new cycle.

Chapter 5: Reading Diagrams

Exercise 1, pages 38-39
1. the nose and the mouth
2. a bronchus
3. a bronchiole
4. alveoli
5. No, there is no major difference.

Exercise 2, pages 40-41
1. the epidermis
2. the dermis
3. the dermis
4. a hair
5. a pore
6. The body cools.
7. Less blood flows to the skin, so the blood does not lose heat.
8. The skin is an organ that cools the body when it is hot and keeps the body warm when it is cold.

Exercise 3, page 42-43
1. greenstick   4. multiple
2. compound   5. simple
3. comminuted

Unit 1 Review–Human Biology, pages 44-45
PART A
1. tiny pieces of food and bacteria
2. (3)   This sentence includes the most important details in the paragraph.
3. 3, 4, 2, 1
PART B
1. the enamel and the dentin
2. blood vessels and nerves
3. the enamel
4. the dentin and the enamel

Unit 2: Plant Biology

Chapter 6: Restating Facts

Exercise 1, pages 50-51
PART A
1. (b)   3. (c)   5. (d)
2. (e)   4. (a)
PART B
1. (d)   3. (b)   5. (c)
2. (e)   4. (a)   6. (2)

Exercise 2, pages 52-53
PART A
1. (c)   3. (a)   5. (d)
2. (e)   4. (b)   6. (1)
PART B
Answers may vary. Use these answers as a guideline.
1. Many useful medicines are made from plants.
2. Quinine, a medicine that is used to treat malaria, comes from the bark of the cinchona tree.
3. Morphine, a drug that kills pain, comes from the dried sap of a poppy.
4. Creams that soften the skin often contain oil from the leaves of the aloe vera plant.
5. (3)

Exercise 3, pages 54-55

Answers may vary. Use these answers as a guideline.

PART A

1. Cactuses can survive without much water because of their special features.
2. Lots of water can be stored in the cactus plant's wide stems.
3. The plant's thick skins hold in water.
4. Cactus roots are long, but they do not grow deep.
5. The roots catch rainwater quickly.

PART B

1. Sap, the liquid in plant roots and stems, can be made into many different things.
2. Chewing gum is made from the sap of the sapodilla tree.
3. The maple syrup we eat on pancakes comes from the sap of sugar maple trees.

Try It Yourself! page 55

The celery stalk in water should stay stiff longer. This is because the stalk in water can soak up extra water, while the other stalk loses water.

Keeping the leaves on the stalks should cause the water in the celery to evaporate (dry up) more quickly. This is because water in the celery evaporates mostly from tiny holes on the underside of the leaves.

If you added food coloring to the water, you are able to see the path that water and other nutrients travel through the plant.

Chapter 7: Comparison and Contrast

Exercise 1, pages 58-59

You should have placed an X in the following columns.

1. Both
2. Giant Sequoia Tree
3. Redwood Tree
4. Both
5. Redwood Tree
6. Giant Sequoia Tree
7. Giant Sequoia Tree
8. Both

Exercise 2, pages 60-61

You should have place an X in the following columns.

1. Both
2. White Water Lily
3. Water-Fern
4. Both
5. Water-Fern
6. Both
7. White WaterLily
8. White Water Lily
9. Water-Fern
10. White Water Lily
11. White Water Lily
12. Water-Fern
13. Both

Exercise 3, pages 62-63

PART A

You should have placed an X in the following columns.

1. "Flier" Seeds
2. "Hitchhiker" Seeds
3. Both
4. "Hitchhiker" Seeds
5. Both
6. "Flier" Seeds

PART B

You should have placed an X in the following columns.

1. Plants
2. Both
3. Plants
4. Animals

Try It Yourself! page 63

The leaves smeared with petroleum jelly cannot "breathe" as they need to. They will probably wither and finally die. This shows that leaves must be able to breathe to survive.

Chapter 8: Classifying

Exercise 1, pages 66-67

PART A

Category	Female Flower Part	Male Flower Part
Name	pistil	stamen
What It Produces	eggs	pollen
Includes	1. ovary 2. style 3. stigma	1. stalk 2. anther

PART B

Category	Wind-Pollinated Flowers	Insect-Pollinated Flowers
Features	1. no scent 2. no petals	1. sweet scent 2. colorful petals
Examples	1. grass 2. shade trees	1. orchids 2. wild roses 3. sunflowers 4. daisies

Exercise 2, pages 68-69

Category	Tundra	Mediterranean	Grassland
Location	Far north of the equator and in Asia (in the mountains)	Around the Mediterranean Sea; in parts of California, South America, and Australia; in northern Africa	Australia, South America, central United States, and central and southern Africa
Weather	Cold and windy all year	Warm, wet winters and hot, dry summers	Hot summers and cold winters
Soil	Frozen	Warm	Frozen in winter and warm in summer
Plants that grow there	1. Grasses 2. Mosses 3. Dwarf trees, such as the arctic willow	1. Evergreen shrubs and trees with needles, such as the digger pine 2. Evergreen shrubs and trees with leaves, such as the scrub oak	1. Grasses 2. Trees

Exercise 3, page 70

Category	Desert Plants	Saltwater Plants
Features	1. can store large amounts of rainwater 2. have thick skins to keep water from evaporating	1. have hollow spaces to store air
Examples	1. cactus	1. sargassum 2. kelp

Try It Yourself! page 71

A *fruit* is the ovary of a flowering plant. A fruit contains one or more seeds. Your list of fruits may include oranges, apples, grapes, melons, bananas, tomatoes, peppers, squash, eggplant, cucumbers, beans, peas, and nuts.

A *vegetable* is a stem, leaf, or root that is eaten. It does not contain seeds. Your list of vegetables may include lettuce, cabbage, spinach, broccoli, cauliflower, onions, potatoes, turnips, carrots, and garlic.

In addition, grapes, oranges, and watermelons are fruits that have seeds naturally, but can be bought without seeds.

Chapter 9: Drawing Conclusions

Exercise 1, pages 74-75

Answers for questions 6–10 may vary. Use these answers as a guideline.

1. Yes. Parasites get the water they need from their hosts.
2. No. A partial parasite must have a host.
3. Yes. Suckers pull water from the host.
4. Yes. To produce its own food, a plant must have leaves and chlorophyll.
5. No. Mistletoe helps some animals, but it does not help its host.
6. Mistletoe can make some of its own food because it has leaves and chlorophyll.
7. Parasites may destroy the crops that the farmers hoped to sell.
8. Parasites do not make their own food. They tap into the stems and roots of other plants and steal food.
9. No. Parasites need host plants to give them food.
10. **Alike:** All plants need food to survive.
    Different: Parasites cannot make all the food they need to survive, while other plants can.

Exercise 2, pages 76-77

Answers for questions 8–10 may vary. Use these answers as a guideline.

1. Yes. Cats are playful when they are around catnip.
2. No. Gardeners plant catnip to control insects.
3. Yes. Insects stay away from catnip.
4. No. Insects avoid catnip.
5. No. Some people plant catnip to keep insects away.
6. Yes. Scientists are continuing to learn about catnip.
7. No. The passage says nothing about how the smell affects people.
8. A cat would probably react with excitement after being away from catnip for a few hours.

9. No. When a cat smelled catnip, it would probably try to rub against the plant and chew it. Therefore, catnip would not grow well around cats.
10. The ant would probably go around the drop of oil to reach the food. The ant would avoid touching the catnip oil.

Exercise 3, page 78

1. No. The passage says that *some* trees can reproduce in more than one way. It is not reasonable to conclude that *all* trees can do this.
2. Yes. The passage says that most trees bear flowers. These flowers produce seeds.
3. No. The information in the last paragraph tells you this conclusion is not correct.
4. Yes. Apple trees "sometimes" sprout from green shoots, but this is not the common way that new apple trees grow.
5. by bearing flowers with seeds
6. from seeds or from shoots sprouting from their roots
7. Both trees can reproduce from green shoots.

Try It Yourself! page 79

The seeds that soaked in warm water and were left in a warm place should start to grow first. The seeds placed in the refrigerator will probably not sprout. The seeds kept at room temperature will grow, but more slowly than the seeds left in a warm place.

You can draw the conclusion that seeds do not sprout during the winter in many places because the weather is too cold. Seeds need to grow in warm places.

Chapter 10: Diagrams

Exercise 1, page 82

Answers may vary. Use these answers as a guideline.

1. A smooth leaf has a smooth edge, but all the other leaves have jagged edges.
2. A toothed leaf has small jagged points around its edge.
3. A lobed leaf does not have jagged points, but its outline curves in and out.
4. A lobed-toothed leaf has both teeth (small jagged points) and lobes (a curved outline).

Exercise 2, page 83

1. lobed-toothed   3. toothed
2. smooth   4. lobed

Exercise 3, page 84

1. (3) There are about 20 growth rings circling the tree.
2. (4) The diagram and the passage describe the location of sapwood.
3. (1) Trees need food to live. Since bark carries food to the various parts of the tree, bark helps to keep the tree alive.

Unit 2 Review—Plant Biology, pages 86-87

1. (1) Choices (2), (3), and (4) retell only one detail.
2. (2) Many humans use certain animals as food.
3. (3) All plants, including carnivorous plants, make their food by photosynthesis.
4. (2) This word is explained in paragraph 2.
5. (2) Carnivorous plants eat insects for some of their food.
6. (1) The passage describes the unusual movement of the Venus flytrap.

Unit 3: Physics

Chapter 11: Identifying Facts and Opinions

Exercise 1, page 92

1. O   3. F   5. F
2. F   4. F   6. O

Exercise 2, page 93

1. (1)   2. (4)   3. (11)

Exercise 3, page 94

1. O   5. F   9. F
2. O   6. F   10. F
3. F   7. F   11. F
4. F   8. F   12. O

Smooth surfaces (plastic, for example) create the least friction. The car will move the farthest when the surface is smooth. A heavy-weight car will move farther than a light-weight car. This is because the heavier weight has greater force.

Chapter 12: *Making a Hypothesis*

Exercise 1, pages 98-99

1. (3) The other statements are not reasonable hypotheses for the following reasons: There was no evidence to support choice (1). If choice (2) were true, the rest of her body should feel warm too, not just her hands. Choice (4) would not explain why her hands were getting warm.

2. (1) The other statements are not reasonable hypotheses for the following reasons: There was no evidence to support choice (2). Choice (3) seems unlikely, since most substances can become warm. Choice (4) would not explain why her hands remained cool.

3. (3) The other statements are not reasonable hypotheses for the following reasons: If choice (1) were true, it would not explain why the thermometer always showed warmer temperatures closer to the ceiling and cooler temperatures closer to the floor. Choice (2) would not explain what Nan observed. She was measuring only indoor temperatures. If choice (4) were true, the warmer air would have been near the floor.

4. (2) The other statements are not reasonable hypotheses for the following reasons: If choice (1) were true, there would not have been a difference in temperature when Nan first measured. Choice (3) would not explain the change that Nan observed after she turned on the fan. Choice (4) would not explain the fact that Nan

had been able to measure differences in temperatures.

5. (2) None of the other statements explain why Lucy could not lift the suitcase from the ramp but could push it up the ramp.

Exercise 2, pages 100-101

1. (3) The most logical guess is that Rose had packed ice cubes, but she had not put them in a plastic bag.

2. (2) The passage explains that it was a hot day and the trip was long.

3. (4) Nothing in sentence 7 describes the hot weather.

4. (3) He was wiping off the parts because he thought they were dirty.

5. (2) He would change the battery if he thought the old battery was dead.

Exercise 3, pages 102-103

1. Cal had been using the laptop.
   Evidence: The top of the laptop was warm.

2. The heat from the cup had made the top of the laptop warm.
   Evidence: Cal said he had put the cup of hot chocolate on top of the laptop.

3. Cal must have been using the laptop after all.
   Evidence: An insulated cup stays cool.

4. The telephone wires expanded (became longer) in the heat.
   Evidence: The wires were sagging more than usual.

5. A car uses more gas when it moves uphill against the pull of gravity than when gravity helps push it downhill.
   Evidence: The campground was high in the mountains (so the trip to the campground was uphill and the trip home was downhill).

Try It Yourself! Page 103

When the bottle sat in a pan of very hot water, the balloon filled with air. This is because the hot water makes the air in the bottle expand. The expanded air uses more space, so it fills up the balloon.

When the bottle sat in a bowl of ice water, the balloon got smaller. This is because the ice cools the air in the bottle. Cold air needs less space, so all the air moves out of the balloon and back into the bottle.

Chapter 13: The Scientific Method

Exercise 1, pages 106-107

1. (4)   3. (2)
2. (2)   4. (1)

Exercise 2, pages 108-109

Answers may vary. Use these answers as a guideline.

1. Why does the tile floor feel cold when the rug does not?
2. Heat can be conducted, and some materials conduct heat better than others.
3. The tile feels cold because it conducts heat better. The tile carries away body heat faster than the rug does.
4. He put one can of boiling water on the tile and another can on the rug. Then he compared the cans to see which one cooled off more quickly.
5. He concluded that his hypothesis was correct—the tile conducted heat better than the rug did.

Exercise 3, page 110

1. c   3. a   5. b
2. e   4. d

Try It Yourself! Page 111

The answers to steps 3, 4, and 5 are not the only possible answers. All answers should be carefully thought out and reasonable.

1. How does sound change when you change the instrument making the sound?
2. Sound changes when the instrument changes.
3. A bigger instrument makes a lower sound.
4. Fill 8 glasses with different amounts of water. Tap the glasses. Compare the sounds made by the different glasses.
5. The hypothesis was correct: The glass with the most water makes the lowest sound.

Unit 3 Review–Physics, pages 112-113

1. a. O; b. F; c. F; d. O
2. (2)   4. (4)
3. (3)   5. (2)

Unit 4: Chemistry

Chapter 14: Cause and Effect

Exercise 1, pages 118-119

1. **Effect:** People often became sick, and many died.
2. **Cause:** The milk contained bacteria.
   Effect 2: Bacteria caused deadly diseases.
3. **Effect:** The bacteria in the milk were killed.
4. **Cause:** Almost all milk is now pasteurized.
   Effect 2: Milk is no longer a dangerous drink.

Exercise 2, pages 120-121

1. **Effect:** The liquid eggs become a solid. OR The proteins in the eggs are denatured.
2. **Cause:** Egg whites are mixed with an acid.
3. **Cause:** Key limes grow only in the Florida Keys.
4. **Effect:** Key lime pie was invented after 1856.
5. **Cause:** The citric acid in key limes can denature the eggs, without heat.
6. **Effect:** Modern recipes for key lime pie call for cooking.

Exercise 3, page 122

1. **Cause:** Bonds are like glue.
2. **Effect 1:** Glue molecules stick together tightly.
   Effect 2: Glue molecules stick tightly to other substances.
3. **Cause:** Solvents can break the bonds between molecules. OR
   Solvents can break the bonds between the glue molecules on a price sticker and the molecules of an item.

Try It Yourself! page 123

Substances such as dish soap and fruit juice combine with water to make a solution. Once these substances have been added to water, you will never again have just water and just dish soap or fruit juice.

Substances such as sand and cooking oil are mixtures. Although these substances mix quickly with water, they soon separate. After some time, you will once again have just water and just sand or cooking oil.

Chapter 15: Predicting Outcomes

Exercise 1, pages 126–127

1. (1) The passage does not mention the color of recycled paper. But it does say that recycled paper is not strong.
2. (2) Paper fibers separate when they are soaked in water. The plastic coating keeps water from soaking into the paper.
3. (1) Stores try not to spend more than they need to. Recycled paper should be cheapest. The sign would not need to be strong, so signs are a good use of recycled paper.
4. (3) New fibers will strengthen the envelopes.

Exercise 2, pages 128–129

1. The soil is alkaline.
2. The peat moss will help the acid-loving azaleas but hurt the alkaline-loving clematis.
3. The crop will probably be small.
4. Debra should add both compost and peat moss. The peat moss will raise the acid level in the soil. The compost will help the sandy soil hold water.

Exercise 3, page 130–131

1. (2) Eggs are emulsifiers. They help make the mixture smooth.
2. (4) The flavor will change, but the quality will not.
3. (3) Gelatin is a stabilizer. It keeps ice crystals from forming.

Try It Yourself! page 131

Oil and water tend to separate from each other. That is because the oil molecules naturally stick together and do not mix for long with water. Detergent emulsifies the oil. It breaks the oil up into smaller drops so the oil stays mixed longer with the water. Detergent helps clean dirty dishes by breaking up the oils in many foods.

Chapter 16: Charts

Exercise 1, pages 134–135

1. It strengthens bones and teeth.
2. magnesium
3. milk and milk products; dark-green leafy vegetables
4. sodium chloride
5. salt
6. calcium and phosphorus
7. phosphorus and sulfur
8. They strengthen bones and make hair and nails.

Exercise 2, pages 136–137

1. (3)   3. (1)   5. (2)
2. (2)   4. (1)   6. (4)

Exercise 3, pages 138–139

1. It will be flat, and it will no longer have paint on it.
2. 80 years or more
3. Its shape may be different, but it will still be intact.
4. $500 - 5 = 495$ years (This is an estimate.)
5. When cans are recycled, they are not filling up a dump.
6. Styrofoam never decomposes. It will always be in the dump.
7. a paper milk carton
8. Natural substances decompose more quickly than manmade substances.

Unit 4 Review–Chemistry, pages 140–141

PART A

1. **Effect:** The water becomes acid and makes acid rain.
2. **Cause:** Acid rain changes the soil.
3. (1)

PART B

4. It is damaging ancient buildings and statues.
5. It has killed most of the fish and many plants and other animals.
6. The Chinese have many health problems, such as pneumonia.

Unit 5: Earth Science

Chapter 17: Identifying Problems and Solutions

Exercise 1, pages 146–147

1. (2) 3. (1) 5. (1)
2. (3) 4. (3)

Exercise 2, pages 148–149

1. (4) 3. (1) and (2)
2. (3) 4. (3)

Exercise 3, pages 150–151

1. (2) 2. (1)

3. Many people live in small villages, and they may not have TVs or e-mail.
4. They do not know which earthquakes will cause tsunamis.

Chapter 18: Using Prior Knowledge

Exercise 1, pages 154–155

1. (4) This term is explained in paragraph 2.
2. (2) Most earthquakes happen where tectonic plates meet. In an earthquake, the ground shakes. Buildings shake as well. If a building can sway with the ground, it is less likely to be damaged.
3. (4) You would need to consider both how often the earthquakes occur and how strong they are. With this information, you could build a skyscraper that would be more likely to survive an earthquake.
4. (4) The volcano lies where two tectonic plates meet. The plates may move again, causing another eruption or an earthquake. Nothing in the passage suggests that plates ever stop moving.

Exercise 2, pages 156–157

1. (4)   3. (1) and (4)
2. (2) and (3) 4. (2)

Exercise 3, pages 158–159

1. (2) Water must evaporate before clouds can form.
2. (3) The two weather conditions that lead to hail are found most often in spring. This means it is likely there will be more hailstorms in spring than in other seasons.
3. (3) A strong upward draft keeps hailstones from falling. As long as they keep bouncing up, they keep getting bigger.
4. (1) An ocean has large amounts of water than can be evaporated. In a warm climate, the Sun warms the water, and then the water evaporates. This causes rain.

Try It Yourself! Page 159

The cold air from the ice cubes and the hot, moist air inside the jar collide. This causes drops of water to form on the inside of the jar. This is how rain and fog form.

Chapter 19: Line Graphs

Exercise 1, pages 162–163

1. (4) The label on the left says "Billions of People."
2. (1) The label at the bottom says "Year."
3. (1) The line moves up only very slightly between the years 100 and 1100.
4. (3) The point for the year 1700 is below the 1 billion line.
5. (2) The point for 1800 is on the 1 billion line.
6. (2) Between about 1300 and 1400, the line goes down slightly. That is the only time the line goes down.

7. (4) The point for the year 2000 is on the 6 billion line.
8. (4) The line is almost flat until the year 1700. At that point, the line curves up sharply. The dotted line after 2000 shows that scientists estimate the population will continue to increase rapidly.

Exercise 2, pages 164-165
1. June and July
2. February and November
3. June
4. December
5. about 11 hours
6. 10 hours
7. 4 hours
8. April
9. before
10. 6 months

Exercise 3, pages 166-167
1. 1960
2. 1970
3. about 230 million tons
4. It has gone up steadily.

Chapter 20: Bar Graphs

Exercise 1, pages 170-171
1. (3)   2. (2)
3. Asia
4. Australia
5. South America
6. (g)   10. (c)
7. (d)   11. (f)
8. (a)   12. (e)
9. (b)
13. Australia is a flat country.

Exercise 2, pages 172-173
1. (e)   3. (d)   5. (b)
2. (a)   4. (f)   6. (c)
7. 1998
8. 2006
9. 2001 and 2003
10. seven years (1996, 1999, 2000, 2002, 2004, 2005, and 2006)
11. (2)

Exercise 3, pages 174-175
1. (e)   3. (d)   5. (b)
2. (c)   4. (a)
6. November and December
7. July
8. about 2½ inches
9. April
10. Summer. The lowest amounts of precipitation are during the months of June, July, and August.

Unit 5 Review–Earth Science, pages 176-177
PART A
1. to kill insects
2. DDT kills other animals too.
3. passed a law forbidding the use of DDT
4. because DDT kills malaria-spreading mosquitoes
5. DDT that was used as an insecticide.
PART B
1. the United States—its bar is the highest
2. about 175 gallons per person per day
3. Kenya—its bar is the lowest
4. about 13 gallons per person per day